HEDON AND HOLDERNESS

Words by
JOHN MARKHAM

Illustrations by
MYRTLE J. BARTER

Highgate Press (Markham) Limited
1994

British Library Cataloguing in Publication Data.
A catalogue record for this book is available from the British Library.

Copyright © Text by John Markham, 1994
Copyright © Illustrations by Myrtle J. Barter, 1994

ISBN 1 899498 00 1

Published by
Highgate Press (Markham) Ltd.
24 Wylies Road, Beverley, HU17 7AP
Telephone (0482) 866826

Produced by

4 Newbegin, Lairgate, Beverley, HU17 8EG
Telephone (0482) 886017

Cover Picture: No. 49 bus at Hedon crossroads

Contents

	Page
Preface	iv
Acknowledgements	v
Brought up in a Borough	1
Hedon in Wartime	5
The Streets of Hedon	11
Sheriff Highway	15
Lambert House	18
Hedon Churches and Chapels	22
Goody Shops	27
Wearing Well	30
Entertainment	33
Going to Hull	36
Paull – Somewhere to go	40
Inns of Hedon and Holderness	44
Stanley Wilson – M.P. for Holderness	49
Little Humber – *Back of Beyond*	53
Home Cooking	56
Holderness Talk	59
Holderness Churches	61
Burton Constable Hall	67
Withernsea	70
Spurn Point	75
The Reluctant Rector – Dr. John Hymers	79
A Holderness Murder	82
Winifred Holtby and *South Riding*	84
Postscript	90

Preface

This is a self-indulgent book in which I have chosen to write about people and places which have significance and interest for myself. But, although it is largely a book of personal impressions and opinions, it is not an autobiography for it would be presumptuous to imagine that anyone would have any interest in the story of my life.

Neither is it a history of the area, although it includes the historical background to some of the subjects, information which I have learnt over a longish period and which has added a new dimension of understanding to the affection for Hedon and Holderness which I have had from my childhood.

Early memories and impressions are the dominant theme, for that is the time when perception is clearest and attitudes are formed which no later experience or knowledge can dint. Some of these opinions are, inevitably, critical, but I hope they will be judged in context and not cause offence. My aim throughout has been to convey the love I feel for the area where I was born and brought up – a decision of Destiny with which I have few complaints.

John Markham
October 1994

Acknowledgements

Many people have assisted in the preparation of this book and, in particular, I want to thank my artist collaborator, Myrtle J. Barter, who took up with great enthusiasm my idea of a co-operative venture and with whom it has been a pleasure to travel round Holderness visiting the places I was keen for her to illustrate. The results speak for themselves. This is a book of words *and* pictures and Myrtle's delightful illustrations are an integral part of the whole.

I am grateful to Mrs. Joan Fielding of Westwood Typewriting Services who worked so efficiently and quickly in the unreasonably short time I asked her to type the manuscript, and to Barry Sage and Barry Ireland of B.A. Print for once again doing far more than any author or publisher has the right to expect of a printing firm. Father Dominic Minskip kindly allowed me to quote from his article, 'The Catholic Mission of Nuthill and Hedon in the Eighteenth and Nineteenth Centuries' in *Four Essays in Yorkshire Catholic History* (1994) and Mr. John Morris, Headmaster of Hymers College, generously allowed me to reproduce Herbert Ballard's photograph of the portrait of Dr. John Hymers. Hedon Town Council has kindly granted permission for the reproduction of the Town Crest and the churchwardens of St. Margaret's Church, Hilston, also kindly allowed me to reproduce an illustration from the guide to the church.

The launch of this book in Hedon has been made possible by the help and support of Councillor Alan Bucknall, Mayor of Hedon, and Mr. Martin Craven, Treasurer of the Hedon Museum Society and a friend and fellow historian, who also generously allowed me to reproduce photographs from his extensive Hedon collection.

I hope that this book will be of some help to them in their determination to foster interest in the history of Hedon and the establishment of a museum.

Brought up in a Borough

We were brought up knowing that we lived in a borough, not a mere village, and, although we were not sure what a borough was, we felt very superior when we saw that the mace carried in front of the Mayor of Hedon was grander than the one preceding the Lord Mayor of Hull.

There seemed to be a never-ending sequence of processions and parades, the climax of special weeks to encourage national savings (like 'Save the Soldier' and 'Wings for Victory'), all beginning at the Town Hall and taking the longest possible route round the little town to give everyone a chance to see the spectacle before they arrived at St. Augustine's Church, the King of Holderness, to pray for peace.

Borough politics tended to attract extroverts with more than average self-confidence and, like many politicians, they fully discharged their public duties merely by providing us with an endless source of amusement. Their processions exposed them cruelly to the disrespectful and sometimes ribald comments of spectators. 'Like a lot of owd sheep,' one farmer muttered as they waddled along, and, when the grand occasion was abruptly ended by a heavy shower, he added, 'This rain'll do a lot more good than that there parade ever will.'

On the same afternoon there was great apprehension when the woman who collected the rates (and walked with her employers in order to inflate their numbers) suddenly left the procession. The drama subsided when it was explained that,

Hedon Town Hall, St. Augustine Gate, built in 1693 by Henry Guy, M.P. My great grandfather, Howard Markham, sergeant at mace and hall keeper, lived here with a large family which needed to spread into the attic — so I claim this as my ancestral home.

Havenside. The Haven was the waterway which brought Hedon into being. Infilling in recent years has removed important reminders of Hedon's great days as a medieval port.

feeling something was not quite right, she had put her hand to her mouth and realised she had forgotten to replace her false teeth.

Elections were suspended for the duration of the war, vacancies were filled by nomination, and those who got in without the voice of democracy being heard were sneered at for having 'just crept in', a description which I thought meant they had entered the Council chamber on all fours.

Apart from the accompanying policeman who guarded their processions from physical onslaught, there were three who wore special clothes to designate their office and status, all, in fact, Georgian costumes: the Sergeant at Mace in a black silk topper and coat with shoulder cape, the Town Clerk in wig and gown, and the Mayor in tricorn hat and fur-edged bright-red robe which revealed inches of trousered leg if he was tall or which almost trailed the ground if he was tiny. The other councillors and aldermen had no insignia of office until one Mayor purchased scarves – yellow and blue, I think – which they wore knotted round their necks and overlapping their shoulders so that they looked like overgrown boy scouts.

There was only one woman member. She wore a fur coat and walked with a limp and, in spite of the humour the Council inspired, it was considered very bad taste when all the civic dignitaries were impersonated in an amateur concert to the delight of everyone but the prototypes and one performer limped on stage as the fur-coated councillor. Years later this amateur actress became Mayor herself and her attempts at public speaking have provided another generation with huge hilarity.

Elected councillors in the years before the war were mostly members of the Hedon establishment, and a pioneering feminist outsider had not been successful when she attempted a break-through. It was customary on election nights for the upper windows of the Town Hall to be 'thrown open' – the phrase that was always used and which suggested something far more dramatic than a mere opening. After the results had been announced the candidates spoke in order of priority, first the one who topped

Kilnsea Cross, Holyrood House, has only a chance connection with Hedon. It originally stood at Ravenser and is thought to have commemorated the landing there in 1399 of Henry Bolingbroke, later Henry IV. Costal erosion forced it to be moved further inland to Kilnsea and it was eventually taken to Burton Constable by the Constables, Seigneurs of Holderness. James Iveson, their lawyer and all-powerful Town Clerk of Hedon, acquired it and erected it here in the 1820s.

the poll, and last the most ignominiously defeated. The woman who had attempted to join their ranks was the final speaker, but the democratic mauling had not ended in her humiliation. 'Defeated but undaunted!' she yelled in revolutionary words which became an endlessly repeated family joke and, for all I know, was handed down in many other Hedon households.

The fine Town Hall we took for granted. During the war the impressive court room served a more utilitarian role as the distribution place for ration books and the building itself was the Civil Defence headquarters with the siren to wail out the start and end of air raids on its roof. Only long after the war was it revealed that the Town Hall contained a consignment of fold-up cardboard coffins, ready to be assembled if a disaster required a mass disposal beyond the resources of the local joiner and undertaker.

As the King of Holderness, St. Augustine's Church was an obvious symbol of our superior status. It was so undeniably the most important church in the area that Hedon people, even the irreligious, took pride in its size – and in some indefinable way felt that they deserved a little of the credit for its importance. In its great days of early medieval prosperity Hedon had three churches. St. Nicholas survives only in the name of a street and in strange bits of stone that surface from time to time in gardens on the site, and the foundations of St. James were obliterated when Lambert Park Road was built.

But there was still the Haven, the natural waterway, as a link with the days when Hedon was a prosperous port. All through the war, and probably after, Humber keels sailed up with cargoes of coal which were unloaded by the crew, as skilfully as performers on a circus tightrope, wheeling heavy barrows on precarious sloping planks from ship to shore. There was Bill Sleat, the boot and shoe repairer and one of Hedon's characters, who kept his 'coggie' boat on the Haven and sometimes rowed it as far as Paull. I never knew why and just assumed it was one of those inexplicable things that adults tended to do. A plain and gloomy Georgian warehouse stood next to the spot where the coal was piled, a barren area impregnated with black dust even after the mounds of coal had been removed in sacks, and a farm nearby bore the name of Harbour Farm. Beyond the Borough Arms, where the grimy keelmen slaked their thirst, was Far Bank, the long, deep, hollowed-out field, by then grass-covered and with a pleasant walk on either bank, but once the

The coat of arms behind The Paddock, Souttergate, is thought to have been used at the celebration of Queen Victoria's Golden or Diamond Jubilee.

West Haven, a man-made adjunct to the natural Haven, dug out as a dock during the short period of expansion when the Haven could no longer cope with the number of ships sailing up to Hedon.

Delight that the Hedon mace was better than the one carried before the Lord Mayor of Hull was a continuation of an ancient feud: Hull was a much more convenient port, particularly as ships became larger, and, as Hull grew, Hedon declined. Even after six and a half centuries there is lingering resentment at the rise of that little upstart, Hull, and the problems it caused. No one has expressed it more strongly than the all-powerful early 19th-century Town Clerk of Hedon, James Iveson, who spoke scathingly of Hull before a committee of the House of Commons: 'It is a place I don't like, nor the people who live there, particularly the burgesses.'

Borough status was granted in 1348 and the tower of St. Augustine's completed long after the great days had passed, but the right to send two M.P.s to Westminster lasted, iniquitously, until 1832. Hedon found consolation for what it had lost by hanging on desperately to every privilege it had ever acquired.

When two Royal Commissioners arrived in Hedon on 30 November, 1833, as part of a national inquiry into local government, they met appalling rudeness from James Iveson, who even questioned their authority, refused to swear on oath that he would answer all their questions (there might be some he would not *choose* to answer) and threatened that if the government 'take anything from us we shall grumble very much and perhaps resist it'.

It was no wonder that the Commissioners retorted: 'They had met with treatment at Hedon such as they had never experienced in any of the five counties through which they had passed.'

Hedon's consciousness of its history remains. It has lost its borough status but it bitterly resents estate agents and broadcasters who have the impudence to refer to the 'village' of Hedon.

A wartime parade of the National Fire Service.   *(By courtesy of Martin Craven)*

Hedon in Wartime

Hedon was never the same after the war. Most people regard 3 September, 1939, as the date separating the past from the present, but world war seemed only to make Hedon more conscious of its identity and importance. There were more public events, the Mayor, S. T. Johnson, seconded from his headmaster's duties to Civil Defence, was more prominent than any of his predecessors, and there were far more reasons for standing in the street and talking to other people. English reticence was irrelevant in a world at war.

Even small children sensed that something was wrong on the evening of 3 September. It had, I think, been a sunny autumn day, but, even on a pleasant evening, it was odd the way neighbours hung around outside, reluctant to leave and probably longing for reassurance. Voices were unusually taut, there was tension behind every banal remark, and fear and terror were not far away. Only 21 years had passed since the Great War and memories were still fresh. Elderly men with one arm or leg were warnings of what was to come, and there were those who coughed until they were exhausted and struggled to breathe. Attack by gas was thought to be imminent and, until complacency gradually returned, a brief visit to a shop without a gas mask was regarded as an insanely hazardous journey. At certain spots there were yellow boards supposed to change colour on contact with gas. One was near the Haven Bridge and I stared at it whenever I passed.

The N.F.S. reviewed by Johnny Warn. *(By courtesy of Martin Craven)*

It was a terrible shock when one day the yellow looked suspiciously green.

An alarm the first night had neighbours scurrying to each other for support. It proved to be a non-event but it was a trial run for what became a nightly routine in 1941. Some precautions were absurdly naïve. As schoolchildren we were taken into a field on Ivy Lane and told that this was where we would go in an air raid: the trees would shelter us from the bombs. Later, reality broke in and we were tested to see how quickly we could reach home if the buzzer sounded. Unsynchronised clocks meant that useless data was accumulated and I remember only one occasion when classes were interrupted by the siren and the rehearsed routine was submerged in panic.

There was, though, a morning when we were in the playground and planes began fighting overhead. Mr. Cox, the teacher in charge, directed us quietly towards the shelter and the rest of the school followed. We stayed there for what seemed a very long time in the musty murk but we were sorry when it ended as it made a splendidly interrupted day. Children are adaptable and find consolation in the gloomiest circumstances. When night raids became regular and serious, a rule was introduced about attendance at school the following day: if the all-clear sounded before a certain time we began, I think, at 10 o'clock, but after the deadline there was no morning school. As the fatal hour approached we silently prayed for the raid to last just long enough. And when bomb blast shattered windows, the unaffected felt envy of those with the proud scars of war.

Pitch-black streets were nothing strange to anyone too young to have much experience of being outdoors after dark but older people frequently fell over unsuspected objects or had badly bruised faces after close encounters with inflexible walls and lamp-posts. As the black-out became more sophisticated and fragile brown paper and drawing pins were replaced by materials which it was now realised would have to last a long time, putting up the shutters at dusk seemed as normal and boring as washing-up.

It was really quite amusing when lorries arrived and took away iron railings and gates, and it was fascinating to watch the pile of old pans, teapots and kettles rising in the window of an empty shop where scrap metal was collected as salvage. The rumour persists that none of this domestic detritus was ever transformed into weapons, and antique objects probably disappeared as unnecessarily as the valuable old books and documents which were patriotically donated to help the war effort. We took for granted the hundreds of troops stationed in and around Hedon, ready to repel the invasion of this tempting stretch of East Yorkshire coast which miraculously never happened but which I now realise must have been a constant worry to grown-ups who did not speak of their fears in front of the children.

A walk along Ivy Lane had often been spoilt by anxiety, a feeling that you were venturing too far

One of Hedon's wartime money-raising efforts – a mile of pennies in St. Augustine Gate.

(By courtesy of Martin Craven)

Not in Hedon, but a typical corner shop in the Second World War.

from familiar territory. It led to the cemetery and to the outer edge of the town which seemed so remote that Victorians had given it the nickname, California, the distant open land that was too far away to attract any but the bravest emigrants. During the war Ivy Lane changed its rural character when it became a large hutted army camp and eventually a place which stirred a different kind of fear as the temporary home of people never seen for many a year in such numbers in Hedon: foreigners.

The Free French were there, bewildered and dazed, soon after the fall of France, and General de Gaulle paid a much needed visit to re-assure them that *liberté, égalité* and *fraternité* had not been lost for ever. It was also a chastening time for Hedon hosts who thought they 'knew' French and found they didn't. Later there were White Russians, men no country wanted, who marched through the streets to their bath house singing in strong bass voices their melancholy Slavonic songs. They made jewellery out of scrap metal, held a Russian Orthodox service in the Church and put on a display of folk dancing and singing on Market Hill. The Russians by this time were on our side and regarded as heroic allies, and there was great support for Mrs. Churchill's 'Aid to Russia' fund. At the end of the war the singing in the streets stopped, and years later it was learnt that the Hedon contingent, like all the rest, had been shipped 'home' to be butchered.

Girls, and some women whose husbands were in

the services, must have found it a heady experience when, out of the blue, hundreds of young men arrived in Hedon with an urge to find something which for a time would assuage the horror of indefinite incarceration in the all-male bleakness of an army camp. An invitation to a family home was a luxurious relief from communal living in a Nissen hut, and friendships were formed which lasted long after the war. Some friendships led to marriage but I also overheard coded conversations about things which could not be discussed openly, and, as in earlier invasions, the influx of newcomers must have helped to rejuvenate and enrich Hedon's genetic mix.

At school we were taught to sing *There'll always be an England.* The chorus was rousing, but when it veered off into the rhetorical

'Red, white and blue,
What does it mean to you?'

and degenerated into the unconvincing optimism of

'Show them you're proud!
Britain's awake,
The Empire too,
We can depend on you,'

it depressed as much as it cheered. I imagine it was part of the Ministry of Information's campaign to keep our peckers up.

The family upheavals and the intense pain caused by compulsory separation made no impact on me and, apart from hoping more and more keenly as the war dragged on that it would soon be over so that we could enjoy the perfect happiness we were continually promised, I was completely uninterested in news from what was strangely described as the 'theatre' of war. Fear of invasion never crossed my mind – luckily, now that I know how near it was and what could have happened, though war did seem to come closer in the bitter winter of 1941, when birds which had never before been seen in Hedon flew in from northern Europe, fleeing, like refugees, from more than the cold. When adults discussed the raids they would often talk of their concern for their children. 'After all, we have had our lives,' they concluded, even though most of them were only in their thirties or forties.

Bombs fell in the fields round about, once on a searchlight unit in Paull Road, and, in the worst disaster of all, a direct hit on houses in Burstwick Road killed several people, among them all the members of a large family except one who was away from home that night. We did not know that in a nearby house, blasted by the bomb, lived the boy who grew up to become the millionaire Lord White of Kingston upon Hull.

Hedon people were thankful for the five miles separating them from Hull when they watched a night sky overpowered by the fiery red and orange glow from the city in flames. On the warm May evening which ended the following day I suddenly realised that I was not immortal. If there was a raid that night I would not be immune.

Hedon was honoured with a fleeting royal visit when King George VI and Queen Elizabeth passed through on their way to put heart into the people of badly blitzed Hull. I was at school, and it was fairly late in the morning when someone came into the classroom and whispered loudly to the teacher, who then passed on the unbelievable news that we were going out to see the King and Queen. Their whereabouts were meant to be a closely guarded secret but local officials and police had to be given some advance information and I suppose that it was the schoolmaster-mayor, S. T. Johnson, who revealed the highly confidential news. Television has brought Royalty in their most intimate moments into every home, but famous people then lived in another world, and a royal visitor was a remote personnage whom you never expected to see riding in the back of a car along Souttergate.

We went across the playground, down into the air-raid shelter, and, as the school stood on the side of Market Hill, out into Souttergate at street level. It was not long before the King and Queen came past. There was, I feel sure, some escort in front before the royal car went by, probably slowing down a bit but still too fast for more than a fleeting impression. The King was merely a shadowy shape on the far side and he was completely upstaged by the Queen in a pastel outfit, who saw children grouped on the pavement and waved enthusiastically. They had spent the night in a quiet railway siding and I wonder if they were surprised to see how widely their secret movements were known. The police had been told to keep roads clear, inevitably the reason for these precautions were leaked, and the message was quickly passed on. One woman who was quite a character waved her battered handbag at the royal car and shouted, 'Fill it with money!', which in those deferential days was not considered to show the respect with which Hedon should welcome its Sovereign and Consort.

It was an exceptional event but not important enough to be even a nine-days' wonder, and food was the focus of far more lasting interest. There was masochistic reminiscing on lost pleasures: trifles thick with cream, large joints of meat, Fry's chocolate cream and all the things whose absence left what medical experts now explain was the perfect, healthy diet. This was not how it seemed at the time, and, when in the post-war years of even greater austerity a friend saw an American film in which a milkman delivered cream to the house, he was staggered to realise that there were places where such unattainable luxuries were everyday items.

Naturally economical and careful housewives of a puritanical disposition found themselves completely at home with the waste-not want-not philosophy which was now a patriotic theme and which proved they had been right all along. They loved jam-making, bottling fruit, 'putting down' eggs, and reducing the sugar in recipes. Nettles were boiled as a not unacceptable vegetable, mushrooming and brambling acquired added importance and you could earn a few pence by gathering rose hips for the W.V.S. There was, too, bitter denunciation of blackmarketeers and of shop-keepers who had favourites, but few stuck rigidly to their principles when the opportunity of a little extra came their way.

Nostalgia for the war years, which may seem perverse, is really quite understandable, especially as those who look back are the lucky survivors. People then seemed less sophisticated, less cynical. Crowds on Market Hill listened politely to unpolished speakers, felt good when they bought something they didn't really want at a jumble sale, and were amazingly keen to make fools of themselves in public. Fancy dress parades had no difficulty in attracting entrants. One woman of considerable size was presumably so impressed by the generosity of American lease-lend that she draped herself in a white sheet and held aloft a cardboard cone, walking unselfconsciously in procession along St. Augustine Gate and Sheriff Highway as a mobile Statue of Liberty. Rain fell that afternoon but, as a garden party neared its end, a gramophone record was played over a loudspeaker and a solitary middle-aged couple waltzed unsmilingly on the sodden lawn like characters in a Noel Coward play.

Petrol rationing made long walks down the streets and through the fields the normal Sunday outing. It was the extension of Edwardian England when a Hedon weekend formally concluded with a walk to the station to see the last train leave for Hull. There were unavoidable, tedious intervals when you met other family groups but also daring short cuts across private property where I always feared arrest, and the discovery of overgrown rights of way and secret parts of Hedon which parents remembered from their own childhood. The places you know as children make a far deeper impression than anything seen later and this wartime block on the growth of motoring ensured that one more generation had no alternative but to become intimately acquainted with its own surroundings.

The Streets of Hedon

Hedon was an easy place to turn into a plan. All you needed was a ruler to draw straight lines, some down the page and some across, and you had the streets of the town centre. Years passed before I learnt why it was so simple. Purpose-built towns tend to have straight streets, unlike those settlements which develop naturally on the bank of a stream or along a track, and Hedon's grid pattern was the legacy of its creation as a New Town of the Middle Ages.

Not even mentioned in Domesday Book, just over a century later it was one of the country's major ports, created by the Earls of Aûmale ('Albemarle' to the English who could not master the absurdities of French pronunciation), for its Haven led to the Humber and so to the North Sea and the markets of northern Europe.

Hedon's principal thoroughfare was known simply as Main Street, in the American style, and rarely given its official name, St. Augustine Gate. Robert Ellerton, the Post Master, was adamant that it was 'Augustine and not 'Augustine's, and he would be horrified to find the unnecessary 's' now habitually added but the grammatical apostrophe often dropped.

Until the shorter turnpiked Hedon Road was opened in the early 1830s, the only way from Hull into Holderness was over North Bridge, along Holderness Road, through Wyton and Preston to Hedon or beyond. It was a long journey and, for its time, a busy route which had carried some notable travellers in both directions. There must have been excitement or apprehension in 1399 when Henry Bolingbroke returned from exile, landed at Ravenser Spurn and rode with his entourage through the villages of the Holderness Plain to defeat Richard II and claim the throne as Henry IV.

The 17th-century Town Hall made St. Augustine Gate Hedon's Westminster and Whitehall

Souttergate, originally the street of the shoemakers – or more strictly 'those who sewed leather', the route to and from Hull before the opening of the direct Hedon Road in the 1830s.

combined, and the Alison Hall next door, opened in 1931 and used for an assortment of public events and entertainments, increased its status as a social centre. It was not a new role, for in the 18th century, when even towns of minor importance were aping Bath and holding Assemblies, Hedon managed to stage its own Assembly for a few years at the Blue Ball – on a site now occupied by the Alison Hall.

The rules were strict. No gentleman was permitted to dance in his top boots (the equivalent today of waltzing in your wellies), and to avoid the display or development of unseemly attachments partners had to be changed every two dances. The Hedon Assembly reached its glorious climacteric one evening in June, 1798, a time when soldiers were stationed in Holderness to repel the long-threatened French invasion, and it must have been another occasion when Hedon people gawped as theatrically uniformed officers and their ladies descended from their carriages, among them Lady Charlotte Lennox, daughter of the Duke of Gordon, her husband, General Lennox (who later became a duke twice over as Duke of Richmond and Gordon), and Lady Charlotte and Lady Georgina Gordon. And less eminent socially but ultimately more significant were members of a family which was to become famous, a Mrs. and Miss Tennyson, probably the grandmother and great-aunt of the still-to-be-born Poet Laureate, Alfred, Lord.

St. Augustine Gate is really too narrow for a main street, and the nucleus of shops gave it a lively, bustling atmosphere long before modern motorists turned it into a congested danger-zone. Market Place, where the tightly-laced Main Street is able to

W. P. Everingham and Sons, Monumental Masons, Souttergate. A rare survivor of the family businesses which were a feature of Hedon when people lived and *worked in the town.*

The Old Hall, Fletchergate, a building of great architectural importance as an early local example of the Classical style and a fine residence, originally of the Waterlands and eventually of the Fewsons.

breathe out and expand into the pleasant rectangled area (which stretched to the churchyard before infilling with a line of shops). Until recent 'improvements' it had a cobble surface, the only surviving bit of thoroughfare with a top layer of either glacial erratics, debris of Holderness left behind after the Ice Age, or stones used as ballast in medieval ships bringing a light cargo of dried fish from Iceland.

The ornate Georgian Market Cross had been demolished and the weekly Saturday market ended long before I was born, though, by one of the ironies with which history amuses itself, a market has now – controversially – returned. On other days it provides convenient parking space for cars, not carriers' carts, though I think I remember Wright's horsedrawn delivery cart left on the cobbles outside their grocery shop with its shafts pointing at the sky. I *think* I remember, because I have seen it on old postcards, and first-hand experience tends to mingle indistinguishably in the memory with things read and seen and stories repeatedly told by parents and grandparents. It is quite easy to have clear memories of things which happened before you were born.

Hedon, confusingly to strangers, has its Market Hill not far from its Market Place, and why, some time before the 17th century, the Hedon burgesses transferred the town centre from its original site north of St. Augustine's Church to Market Place on its eastern side has never been explained. Market Hill, though it's now a green and semi-rural area unknown to those who speed along the Hull-Withernsea road or use the by-pass, is the heart of

Hedon, the birthplace of the town. By Holderness standards it *is* a hill and, if in your imagination you knock down all the buildings around, you have the rough-land mound on which the Albemarles, Lords of Holderness, created a new community. The name 'Hedon' is from '*heah dun*' – 'uncultivated hill' – the lowest place in England to have attached to its name the hilly *dun*.

The school for the children of freemen tottered to its end in permanent financial crisis and was demolished in 1883, and the cattle pens were left empty, after an epidemic of rinderpest in the 1860s completed the growing trend for dealers to use the railway to send their animals to the larger market in Hull. They lasted long enough to be photographed, but the medieval guildhall and jail exist only in old documents. More recent, and a loss still felt, was the chopping down of the three diseased elm trees which crowned the hill. Previously they were encircled by a wood and iron bull-ring, but the metal was commandeered during the war to melt into munitions and the wooden structure then collapsed.

Market Hill, though denuded of everything which made it a centre of activity, is nevertheless an attractive area when the sun is shining and there is an enticing leafy view along Ivy Lane. It is now a road to executive houses but was a terrifying place on a dark night with blackness all around, the cheerless Victorian vicarage the only refuge against total isolation, and the ghosts of Hedon's dead in the cemetery beyond.

Hedon had its 'gates' on Westlands, rented pasturage on the large communal field, but the 'gate' in the street names simply means 'street'. Souttergate, the street of the shoemakers, or more strictly, of the craftsmen who sewed the leather that was used for clothing as well as footwear, always seemed a long and dreary street, an unpleasant experience to be undergone on your way to and from the station – stuck on the very edge of the town by penny-pinching Victorian investors who wanted the goods yard to be in the adjacent parish of Preston and so avoid payment of Hedon tolls. But, once dull and down-at-heel, it has since been gentrified and is now one of the most important parts of the town with good Georgian houses and cottages on either side, and as genuine a *quartier* of old Hedon as you could hope to find.

Fletchergate, the street of the butchers, is too busy for anyone to linger and savour its history, though it was the street where Rev. John Tickell, who earned a precarious living as a curate and private school proprietor, found the conditions to write his monumental history of Hull published in 1798.

The other gates in Hedon, Baxtergate, Magdalen Gate, St. Nicholas Gate, Swinegate (now George Street) and Walkergate (now Church Lane) have their points of interest but no strong personal associations for me. A street, after all, takes its character as much from the people connected with it as from its architecture. For young children almost every street had its terrifying obstacles to be overcome before you reached safety. There was the harmless old woman we decided was a witch and whose house we ran past to avoid her evil gaze as she stared from a little window where someone claimed to have seen her watching us; the extrovert fireman who stood outside his post with nothing to do but yell out embarrassing and unfunny pleasantries; another old woman who wore a mob cap and had a bright red nose and was known as Mrs. Cherry Nob and who once brought on a storm of terrified tears when she stood next to me in the Post Office; and the gentle giant who would now be called mentally handicapped and who lurched down the streets with a bulging sack where you might end up.

Hedon was only a small place, but it had an inexhaustible supply of comic characters who existed solely for our amusement. Yet there was also this incarnation of evil dangerously close. Familiar streets could be instantly distorted into surrealistic horrors and the walk to and from school turned into a *via dolorosa*.

Sheriff Highway – a fine-sounding name: formerly Mill Lane and called by old residents Paull Road – and even Havenside.

Sheriff Highway

Sheriff Highway always seemed to me a perfectly ordinary name. I never even gave it a thought. It was our address, the road where I was born, and I was amazed when people who heard it for the first time thought it strange. I can now see why.

It's a grandiose name, more appropriate to a multi-lane thruway traversing the United States from east to west than a minor road taking you from the centre of Hedon and leading to Paull and the remoter parts of South Holderness. Older people, I remember, called it Paull Road and, occasionally, Havenside, though Sheriff Highway was only the stretch of road to the Haven Bridge and never included Havenside proper, the turning to the Borough Arms, in spite of claims of current newspaper advertisements which on one memorable occasion have added a bizarre element to the complex subject of Hedon street names by coining a new one – 'Avonside'.

Sheriff Highway took its name from the Sheriff Bridge over the Haven, Hedon's most important bridge, and by the 15th century was known as Sheriff Bridgeway. The bridge – a lifting one – was then to the north of its present position: originally the Haven formed a loop and the crossing was near the junction of Sheriff Highway, Love Lane and Havenside: the wide expanse of roadway there is evidence of the route it naturally followed until it was straightened in the 1770s.

To a young boy walking up and down it twice a day Sheriff Highway seemed a very long road, a long way from school, but it was a pleasant road with overhanging trees from the garden of Holme Garth and the field beyond, and on the other side the greenery of Lambert House. Development had started before the War with the typical Thirties semis of Lambert Park Road, Holme Garth itself, and more semis in a field facing our house. But it was still a country road of fields and animals, and on a summer's morning, when sunshine disappointingly disappeared, it was always a thrill to wait for the moment when the clouds moved away and the sun came silently gliding along Sheriff Highway from the Haven Bridge in the far distance and past Weighbridge House until it reached you and brightened your life.

In the Forties, when cruel winters brought Arctic weather to Hedon, Sheriff Highway was deep in snow which lingered on untrodden ways well into Spring. Then, powerful gusts hurled along the road, bending tall trees hazardously and making eyes smart with dust. 'The winds of March that set my heart a-dancing' — words from a song, *These Foolish Things* – always remind me of Sheriff Highway at that time of year. It was a road where children could safely play, though war made it busier. Only now do I realise how the character of Sheriff Highway would change with the building of army huts in the field occupied by Spencer Close, with more on the site of Haven Staithes, and one in the back garden of a house which had been requisitioned by the military. The world would never have survived if children could not quickly adapt to the most abnormal circumstances, but for older people the arrival of hundreds of strangers with strange accents must have had the impact of a social revolution.

The Haven may have been in its death throes as a commercial waterway, yet it was still a magnet attracting crowds who strolled down Sheriff Highway on an evening to watch the tide come in, a pleasure not to be under-rated. There was always the suspense of wondering what could be carried along by its swell — pieces of cork, bottles, bits of broken baskets and lumps of sodden wood, as well as the tangy, slightly disturbing hint of the sea.

Bending over the parapet of the bridge and staring into the murky straw-strewn water rising higher and higher brought terror and death too dangerously close to be comfortable, but, as the incoming tide reached the top of the steps, there was always a hope that a natural disaster would crown the evening's entertainment. It never did, though I have vague memories of being taken one morning as a very young child to see the flooding in the grassy area alongside the Haven.

Water was the reason for Hedon's existence, and, when the port was in its heyday and activity on and around the Haven was hectic, medieval Sheriff Highway was a far more important thoroughfare than it later became. Standing on land where Lambert Park Road was to be built this century, St. James's, one of the town's three churches, served the many people who lived in this lively part of Hedon, where much of its wealth was created.

Sheriff Highway's oldest recorded name, older even than Sheriff Bridgeway, was Westgate — West Street — an odd name, apparently, to describe a street that was in no way westerly until you realise that it would be the main route, via Havenside, to the man-made West Haven (now Far Bank). Hedon, as everyone knows, suffered a fatal setback when two rival ports, first Ravenser Odd, then Hull, became much more attractive to merchants and shippers, and, by the time the first comprehensive lists of inhabitants and property owners were drawn up, in the late 18th century, Sheriff Highway had resumed the rural tranquillity from which it was just emerging when I appeared on the scene.

In the Georgian and early Victorian periods it was usually known as Mill Lane, on account of its one important building, Charles Gibson's mill, at the corner of Love Lane but originally beside the old unstraightened Haven. The corn mill, with its tower and sails, has gone but the miller's house of 1771 survives as one of Hedon's listed buildings.

In 1795 Mill Lane and Havenside combined had merely a total population of 26, but when, a few years later, John Iveson made his 1804 survey, the southern part had undergone a change even more radical than the alteration of the course of the Haven. From 1802, gangs of brawny men known as bankers had dug out the earth to create the deep, wide Burstwick drain, which bisected fields and crossed Sheriff Highway under a brand new bridge. It was a formidable feat.

Iveson's map shows an early 19th-century Mill Lane bordered on both sides by open fields with such emotive names as St. James and Thorgill Closes, Mrs. Isabell Ombler's Close, and Lady Appleyard's Close. One of these fields, Mr. John Brough's Close, has particular interest for me as it was later bought by my father as land attached to the former Keel Inn which had been built at the end of a row of houses in the 1830s. In the same period the embryo of the later aggrandised Lambert House appeared in a neighbouring field to the north. Although Colonel White's magnificent gardens were long overgrown, his trees flourished in their full maturity, and the view from the back bedroom window as I did my homework in the post-war years is one of my deepest memories, with the paddock fringed on both sides by trees, on the north those of Lambert House, the most beautiful a copper beech, on the south a line of trees in the garden of Sheriff Hall, and, beyond Middle Lane, a team practising on the cricket field.

Lambert House was an L-shaped house in the 1830s, but it was considerably altered later in the century by the White family.

Lambert House

Lambert House is a name with a fine ring to it and there is no doubt it qualifies as one of Hedon's most interesting buildings. Remarkably, too, at a time when historians and conservationists are constantly lamenting the deterioration and demise of buildings whose glory has long departed, Lambert House has never looked better. For me it is a house with many childhood memories of the period when it belonged to the two Misses Emerson, Annie and Tilly, elderly daughters of John Emerson who had previously lived at Twyers Wood and whose best memorial in Hedon is the row of houses on the south side of George Street which he built and which are now regarded by the knowledgeable as fine examples of brickwork. I have been told that when people called at Lambert House he would come to the front door holding a wad of bank notes which he just happened to be counting.

My personal recollections go back only to the final years when Annie and Tilly aspired to run what was fashionably described on a board in the front garden as a country club, a concept which appealed to the Bright Young Things of the Thirties. Again, relying on the overheard comments of adults, I understand that the Emerson sisters, accustomed to good living themselves, provided excellent fare for their paying guests, the grander version of lodgers.

Tilly died in tragic circumstances and Annie was left to soldier on alone in the over-large house which showed painful signs of neglect. She herself lived mainly, I think, in the massive kitchen with its fantastic Eagle range inherited from the previous owners which deserved a final resting place in a museum of social history. She would sit in lonely state at what seemed an enormously long table in the vast, decaying room, reading a newspaper and with a cigarette wedged between her lips, for she smoked constantly and had a deep, husky voice.

William Lambert White, fruit merchant and part-time officer, who was always accorded the title 'Colonel', brought the gardens of Lambert House to perfection. They deteriorated under the Emersons but have now been superbly restored by BP Chemicals Ltd.

She had abandoned all hope of keeping control of the gardens which had been the pride of Colonel White in the late Victorian and Edwardian periods. The central fountain in the Elizabethan garden had long since ceased to flow, and untamed weeds blocked the artistically landscaped streams and waterfalls of the rock garden as impenetrably as the Haven was eventually to be overgrown.

To a child a garden neglected on such a scale was a place of mystery with its own melancholy beauty, and the barely detectable paths where no one walked were silent but unmistakable reminders of a style of life which had become part of history.

During the war Annie Emerson, who had quite a fancy for farming, responded patriotically to the national call to dig for victory and be self-sufficient. The sunken lawn which had been the scene of elegant Edwardian social events now served a more basic purpose. I remember one of Miss Emerson's characteristic comments spoken in her educated but gravelly voice: 'I've got two calves on the sunken lawn.'

Although the house cannot be precisely dated, it is reasonably certain that it was built or re-built somewhere between 1830 and 1840. Its location then would be on a very rural lane with fields all around and its appearance would be very different from the one familiar in later years. It was an L-shaped house, probably of a typical Georgian character: modernisers understandably concentrate on the parts which are most prominent, and the rear of Lambert House retains early 19th-century sash windows.

The house's early history is obscure. Randall Robinson, the builder, appears to have let the property until, in 1865, one tenant, William Thomas White, a Hull merchant and fruit importer, who had already been there four years, found the house sufficiently to his taste to purchase it. A strong trend of English history is for people who have made their money in trade or industry to aspire to transform themselves into landed gentry, and locally there is considerable evidence of wealthy merchants leaving their Old Town houses and moving out to country estates, particularly in the pleasant villages west of Hull. To migrate eastwards was less popular and fashionable, though a corresponding advantage was that one had fewer social rivals. W. T. White cut quite a figure in Hedon public life but it was his son, William Lambert White, successor to his father in 1888, who made the greatest impact on what was now Lambert House, and on Hedon itself.

As well as being prominent in business as a fruit importer, owner of a sugar mill and chairman of a trawling company, he served on Hedon Corporation as councillor and alderman and was three times Mayor. In the late 19th century it became customary for socially ambitious males to join the Victorian equivalent of the territorials, and Mr. W. L. White acquired his proudly used title 'Colonel' through such voluntary service. Bribery and corruption were a traditional feature of Hedon elections and Colonel White, now a landed proprietor, felt it his duty to maintain the feudal responsibilities of men of his class: in the late 1920s, I have been told, he sent a message round to local people instructing them which candidate they should vote for in the council elections.

He died before my time but I heard incessantly about the Whites from Mrs. Florence Mitchell who had been cook at Lambert House and who worshipped the family. She treasured old photographs and menus and described in detail the dishes she had prepared. It was all overwhelming, but now I wish I had listened more carefully.

Mrs. Mitchell's claim that she had been named Florence after Florence Nightingale sounded unlikely but I now know that it was not a common name until Florence Nightingale became a heroine: she was probably right, after all.

Mrs. Mitchell lived to a great age and kept in touch with the White children. One of the sons she frequently mentioned was Dalton (named after his mother, Elizabeth née Dalton) and another was the

White's only daughter (Violet, I think) who married a man with a name famous in shipbuilding and became Mrs. Short. I believe that Mrs. Mitchell received a pension from the Whites during her long years of retirement.

Two particularly interesting features were added to Lambert House during the Whites' occupancy. When G. E. Street restored the south chancel window of St. Augustine's Church in what he believed was the correct Early English style, the stone tracery displaced was re-erected in Lambert House garden. The L-shaped house was enlarged and the missing section of the rectangle completed with additional rooms, one of them the superb folly known as The Dungeon, a bizarre Victorian-Gothic amalgam of stonework and statuary from various local but unidentifiable churches.

The smart white front of the house and the style of its porch are, to me at least, reminiscent of grand residences on the south coast. Whether the Whites were influenced in their alterations by such examples is pure speculation. So, too, is the name of the person responsible for the fine woodwork and ceilings. At that time, James Elwell, a Beverley carver who employed 60 men, was in great demand all over the East Riding. Some of the Lambert House features are similar to proven Elwell work in other houses. It would, in fact, be remarkable if the Whites had not employed the most renowned local firm.

When the war came part of the house was used for Civil Defence, and after the death of Miss Emerson in 1943 the property fell into even greater decline. It was purchased by the East Riding County Council and its days as a residence appeared to have ended. My memories of the garden are largely of this period, particularly of a post-war summer — probably 1947 — when the Hedon Tennis Club was allowed to use the sunken lawn. The weather was glorious, the court surrounded by magnificent trees and it was an idyllic time. Then came an unexpected reversal in the story of decline and fall. In 1948 Lambert House was bought by British Industrial Solvents (later absorbed by BP Chemicals) and its renaissance began. The gardens are once again superb, the reception rooms and the hall are as attractive as they ever were, and modern bedrooms and bathrooms provide comfort and convenience of a quality not enjoyed by the richest Victorians. Lambert House illustrates one of the great themes of English history: to survive one has to adapt to changing circumstances.

St. Augustine's Church, Hedon – the sturdy, masculine King of Holderness.

Hedon Churches and Chapels

Hedon people were proud of their church and took it as a personal compliment that St. Augustine's was the King of Holderness. Its solid four-square tower was a landmark for miles around and the symbol of home as the blue and white Hull Corporation 49 bus neared Salt End and you caught your first reassuring glimpse of its unmistakable shape across the great flat field which had briefly been a racecourse and then an aerodrome: something that never changed whatever else had happened while you'd been away.

Pride in its importance exceeded the obligation to attend its services, though wartime exposure to the precariousness of life temporarily boosted the size of congregations. Early 19th-century plans show the allocation of pews to named parishioners who paid a rent for their reserved seats, the leading residents naturally occupying the orchestra stalls

A neat plaque on the Baptist Chapel, a simple, dignified building, now the premises of the Royal British Legion.

and the nondescripts relegated to their rightful place at the rear and in the side aisles where they could see very little. Perhaps it was some consolation that they missed very little, for ritual and ceremony were kept to the minimum. Hedon was strictly Low Church and remained so under the Vicar, Mr. Ainslie, whose too long tenure from 1903-1942 bridged early Edwardian England and the Second World War in complete oblivion of social and economic change and with no variation of what I later learned was a strict Evangelical style.

Psalms were chanted, and items like the Creed and the Lord's Prayer orated on an uncertain high-pitched note which was impossible to maintain and gabbled at such a speed that you arrived with relief at 'Amen'. One did not kneel to pray but perched uncomfortably on the edge of the polished pine bench with one's head and hand veiling the eyes on the narrow ledge for books, spectacles and gloves. Social trends had diminished the status and strength of the Church of England, but Mr. Ainslie made his own distinctive contribution to the decline of religion in Hedon. Born in India, where his father was an army officer, he was a short, round man, dressed in deepest black, with a shallow, round pork-pie hat of a type worn on the stage by comic curates, and his very white face had a hint of the frostiness which his cold and distant manner conveyed. His services and his preaching, conducted in a monotonous nasal whine, were powerful deterrents to faith.

The overwhelming impression which remains is of greyness, dreariness and cold. There was the colour of stained glass windows but they were the most depressing type of Victorian design with the feeble figures and subdued shades which were thought proper for sacred subjects. An organ and a surpliced choir were no indication of any choral tradition. Some complained of the organist drowning the choir, but he did little harm. The older ones, at least, sang inharmoniously in the strained, unnatural style which is now known as the Anglican hoot. One elderly man boasted that he had never lost his voice though he was in his eighties, and it was true that he could be heard above, and half a note behind, the others, sometimes outdoing the organ, and always out of tune. The ladies of the choir were chastely clad in black gowns and a feminine version of the lozenge-shaped hat like an upturned pin-cushion which used to be worn by archbishops on less formal occasions. An old woman as well up in spirituality as St. Paul insisted that those who allowed the odd curl to protrude were acting contrary to Christian ethics.

Pew rents had long been replaced by collections but the tradition of regular seats remained. A bent, grizzled verger in a black gown who resembled an Old Testament prophet (called by the older people something which sounded like 'Cobby' and which I thought was his title, though it was probably his surname or nickname) handed out prayer and hymn books from a pile near the door and diplomatically moved anyone who, in ignorance, attempted to take over a reserved seat.

Of the regular attenders only one is memorable: an elderly lady, a butcher's wife and, therefore, a person of consequence in the town, who walked in slow, stately steps, stiff and erect, to a front pew. Her coat and dress were ankle-length and her hat was carefully pinned on a coiffure of elaborate white curls. She was, I suppose, a surviving impersonator of the late Queen Alexandra whose distinctive gait, the result of an arthritic leg, caused fashionable ladies to imitate the Alexandra walk.

Most of my memories are of the wartime period and later. There was, I remember, a massive attendance after Dunkirk on a national day of prayer. I ignored the sermon but my mother was impressed and afterwards repeated the Vicar's comparison of Dunkirk with one of the miracles in the Bible, probably the parting of the Red Sea and the delivery of the Jews from Egypt. It was his finest hour.

The Methodist denominations had officially merged in 1932 but there were still separate chapels with their own followers. Methodism to me was unknown territory, and how much sectarian rivalry survived was a subject that never entered my comprehension. Nationally the Wesleyans tended to attract more affluent Nonconformists than

St. Mary and St. Joseph's Catholic Church, Hedon. An attractively simple Georgian building hidden discreetly away behind the priest's house.

Primitive Methodism, and an old neighbour, who herself was C. of E., referred to a relative who had married a 'Prim' in a way which suggested an unfortunate lapse. Some local families were described as 'big Chapel people', and, although antagonism was probably not too serious, ecumenism was barely in embryo, and it was still a matter of conversational interest whether you were Church or Chapel. Less so, though, than in the early years of the century when my father had bragged to another boy that the Church was much bigger than the Chapel; 'But the Chapel's much bigger inside than it is outside,' the boy had answered with a subtextual significance far greater than he realised.

Nonconformists in Hedon apparently had an aptitude for adroit defence of their own brand of religion. In the 1930s a painter and decorator who was also a lay preacher and teetotaller had been spotted up a ladder painting the front of the Queen's Head in St. Augustine Gate, and a passer-by, who thought he had caught a notorious hypocrite *in flagrante delicto*, shouted out triumphantly, 'I'm amazed to see you taking on a job like this.' 'Ah, yes,' said the Methodist painter, 'but, you see, the Devil always settles his debts.'

Everything inside St Augustine's was so solemnly daunting that it was a cultural shock to attend an amateur concert in a Methodist chapel and find people laughing in the same building they used for Sunday services and interspersing prayers and hymns with jokes, comic sketches, jolly songs and tea and cakes. It was all disturbingly informal and cheery, and difficult to believe that this was the same religion as the one practised in the big church just a few yards up the road. Whereas the Vicar did not believe that his brief included social events and entertainment, Chapel people seemed to have an enviable round of diversions. There was something called an Anniversary where prizes were presented, seaside outings (though interrupted by war), and Nonconformist children belonged to an organisation as mysterious and remote as freemasonry called Sons of Temperance, a name I had never seen in writing and which I misinterpreted as the more easily attainable 'Sunday Temperance'.

Hedon had had a Catholic Church since 1803, a neat Georgian building so discreetly situated behind a wall in Baxtergate and with the church and priest's house so subtly integrated that it looked unecclesiastical and succeeded in being as ignored as its founder had intended. The Reverend Joseph Swinburne had established it when no-Popery was still rife, only a few years after the Gordon Riots had triggered off anti-Papist outrages in Hull, and more than 20 years before English Catholics acquired full civic equality with Protestants. He was still in his twenties, had studied in France and been imprisoned for a year during the Revolution, an experience which prepared him to tackle Hedon.

After the Reformation, pockets of Catholicism survived precariously in areas too remote for anyone to take too much notice, and one such district was Holderness, where a number of old farming families, among them the Caleys, the Champneys, the Richardsons, the Robinsons and Wrights, formed a nucleus of Recusants.

Much more important, though, were the Constables of Burton Constable, who had served as M.P.s for Hedon before the Reformation, and who in 1789 had established a Catholic Church at Marton away from the tree-lined lane that led to their stately home, a sophisticated, faintly foreign enclave in the heart of the countryside and just as secluded and as easily missed as the one at Hedon. While they were excluded from Westminster by penal legislation the Constables continued to exert influence behind the scenes in parliamentary elections until the Emancipation Act of 1829 restored their rights and they rapidly supplied a candidate for the next election, the unimpressive but wealthy baronet, Sir Thomas Aston Clifford Constable. Even into the 20th century they practised positive discrimination, preferring to grant tenancies of their farms to Catholics rather than

Protestants. One such farm was Little Humber where my mother was born.

Before Father Swinburne took the brave decision to move to Hedon in 1803, he conducted his services in a small and simple chapel at Nuthill near Preston. No doubt this invasion of Protestant territory caused heads to shake and prophecies to be declared that the day would surely come when Hedon Church itself would be taken over by the Catholics: 'They had it once and they'll have it again.' History is full of surprises and practical jokes, and in more tolerant times St. Augustine's was offered to the Catholics as a temporary venue when their own church was undergoing a major restoration and being divested of certain Victorian embellishments which were considered to be a blemish on its Georgian simplicity.

St. Augustine's was forbidding, but the Catholic Church of St. Mary and St. Joseph was almost frightening, a place where people did things differently. It was *terra incognita,* and people believed that extravagant rites were performed in an incomprehensible language, though few non-members ever attended except as once-in-a-lifetime spectators at a Catholic wedding or funeral, or placed courageous feet on the ground nearby as paying entrants to the Catholic garden party where the quality of the raffle prizes overcame all prejudice.

Catholics encouraged this speculative suspicion by their ghetto-like exclusiveness and the Triumphalist ethos which was dominant until Pope John XXIII sent them, protesting, out of their self-created prison. The priest did not mix with the Vicar and the Methodist ministers, and all one saw of him was a large black unspeaking presence on his occasional journeys to Hull by bus.

Apart from odd remarks about people who fasted before they feasted and who were compelled to give the Church far more than they could afford, sectarian antagonism was rather restrained, though ill-feeling surfaced during the war when many thought the R.A.F. was inhibited from bombing Rome by the proximity of the Vatican. Local Catholics, accustomed to their self-contained community, were also unhappy at being in close proximity to Italian and German prisoners-of-war who now joined their congregation.

Earlier in the century, though, I understood that nominal Anglicans who considered they had done everything sensible that one could reasonably be expected to do by attending morning service were puzzled by these eccentrics who seemed to spend Sunday going backwards and forwards to church. Why on earth didn't they get it all over at one go? There was also the oft-told but possibly apocryphal story of Edwardian schoolboys who put Reckitt's Blue into the holy water stoup so that people emerged from the church with coloured foreheads.

Practical jokes are always tinged with malice and there is no longer the sectarian animosity to inspire such humour — surely a sign of progress.

Market Place, Hedon, until recently the only surviving cobbled area. A town well formerly stood at the southern end (right) and a Market Cross at the northern end (left). The tall block of houses and shops towards the corner of George Street was built 1828-9 by George Sawyer, who gave his name to the street.

Goody Shops

Sweet shops are important in children's lives, often the first lone encounter with a grown-up outside the family network.

It was still possible in the early war years to buy a worthwhile quantity of sweets for a ha'penny, and shopkeepers were prepared to have their dinner-hour interrupted by the tinkle of a doorbell and a customer stocking up for an afternoon at school. Until the war and the opening of a British Restaurant most children, most older people too, went home for their midday meal, and on a hot summer's day, when shop windows were shielded by overhanging canvas shades, returning to school along the deserted Main Street past the Market Place was like walking through a Mediterranean town at siesta.

Mabel Beadle's story-book shop with its pair of

bow-fronted windows always had a wonderful selection of sweets — known in Hedon as goodies. Like other shopkeepers who lived above and behind the shop, she emerged after an interval from some mysterious passage into the small shadowy room. She was always polite, but all grown-ups were old, shopkeepers were very important people, and you were equally respectful and remembered to say please and thank you.

Wright's in the Market Place was even more formal, and little Miss Wright appeared from a back room and briskly greeted you with a no-nonsense 'Yes, thank you,' as she trotted out of view behind bottled boiled sweets drawn up in a line and cornered swiftly to face you at the counter. Button's was near the infants' school and popular, especially as most of the sweets were in boxes on the counter and open to close inspection. I never once heard of anyone stealing anything, never for one minute thought about the possibility; it was a crime beyond human imagination.

Mrs. Barrett's, like Button's, was an all-purpose shop, and, as wartime shortages made sweets a luxury, you were grateful for one of the packets of Victory-V lozenges which had lingered hopelessly on a cardboard dispenser on the wall. Even when rationing was introduced Mrs. Barrett had more stringent regulations for the allocation of sweets than the Ministry of Food considered necessary, and anyone presumptuous enough to ask for a quarter of anything was told quite abruptly, 'You can have two ounce!' We promised ourselves that when the war was over we would never enter her shop again and we gloated over the suffering we would cause. But the end of the war was a long time coming and the end of rationing even longer, and by the time full freedom of choice was restored to the customer Mrs. Barrett had long retired and bitter memories hurt no more.

The sweet shop which differed from all the rest was Freddie Sharpe's. It had a prime position near the crossroads and its original trade was in spare parts for cars and bikes, and other odds and ends. Mr. Sharpe was an alderman and in the Twenties had run a pioneering bus service between Hedon and Hull and his transport business had prospered. For some unknown reason he began to acquire a small stock of sweets, the word spread, and the sideline began to bring in more customers than his original goods.

His dingy, untidy, over-full shop required an author with the descriptive skill of Dickens or Arnold Bennett to do it justice. He had no talent, time or need for window-dressing or display, and decoration and colour were non-existent. Shelves behind the counter were packed tight with shabby cardboard boxes, and the ones which could not find a space were piled in ascending tiers on the treads of the wooden stairs which led to a former bedroom, by then probably turned into a store-room worse than the shop below.

And yet the apparent chaos and disorder were an illusion. Mr. Sharpe knew where everything was, and, when he wanted to favour a customer with a special delicacy he would slip his hand into the right carton, higher than himself, only slightly disturbing the lid, and, like a magician, bring out, almost hidden by his palm, what only he could have known was there. His shop had strange attractions for Italian prisoners-of-war, and he developed his individual style of Anglo-Italian communication, which included such phrases as 'Me no havee'. They must have returned to Italy unjustifiably confident of their command of colloquial English.

It was a time of shortages, of accepting that some things were 'unavailable for the duration', and anyone who dared to behave as though life was normal was given the reminder which stifled any response: 'Don't you know there's a war on?'

Eventually Miss Beadle closed her shop, though there was one memorable Saturday when word rapidly spread that she was open for business, and all the sweets which were no more than pleasant memories were magically on sale again in unlimited quantities. I suppose that during her closure she had been receiving her regular supplies and hoarding them until she considered it worthwhile having a one-day bonanza.

Trade was brisk, the pace grew hectic, and customers' eyes gleamed as they pressed against the counter, as ravenous as prisoners on bread and water who were suddenly offered *haute cuisine:* a foretaste of the wonderful world there would be once the war was over. Everyone bought as much as they could afford but, although there were public promises about making it last, little was left by the end of the day.

Then it was back to Victory-V lozenges.

Wearing Well

High fashion by-passed Hedon and most people wore clothes to cover their nakedness and keep them warm: coats and suits were regarded as fixed assets. The ultimate accolade of anything new was a favourable estimate of its longevity. 'It will wear well,' and, 'It won't show dirt,' were ominous reminders that no replacements could be expected for a very long time, and children flapped around, awkward and embarrassed, in jackets and coats that hung too low, with sleeves that half-covered their hands, and short trousers that shaded knees and most of their calves, not really convinced by repeated assurances that they would soon 'grow into them'.

Strict demarcation was still made between clothes worn on weekdays and those kept for best, though there was an intermediate stage for housewives who changed into something nicer mid-afternoon, once the bulk of their dirtiest jobs were completed.

'They also serve who only stand and wait'.

Very few adults, few children too, went out without a hat or cap, and no woman would have dreamt of attending church with uncovered head. During the war many were directed into war work, and head scarves folded into turbans became popular both on and off duty, a style made classless when it was worn by Mrs. Winston Churchill. In the morning when they cleaned the grate, scrubbed the door-step and polished the brass letterbox and knocker many wore unflattering mob caps, with ugly grips and curlers protruding and disturbing the shape of the hair. More dressy, though, was a halo hat, the kind favoured by the Queen, who had even been seen wearing one as she drove with the King along Souttergate and St. Augustine Gate on a wartime visit to Hull.

My great-aunt, who had been a nanny, had her bedroom cupboards and drawers full of clothes which would have been welcomed by any museum of costume. Several starched nursing aprons which reached her ankles were still in regular use, and she had a whole range of decorative trinkets reserved for going out. A fox fur worn round her shoulders had the animal's flattened face dangling sadly at one end, and a flimsy muslin scarf pinned daringly round the throat was rather naughtily referred to as a fascinator.

No one said strumpets, but the few who made a daring sally – virtually all female – into the world of fashion were so conspicuous that they provided an interesting, novel subject of critical conversation. One woman alternated between two pairs of shoes with heels so much higher than was considered necessary that her friends swung round excitedly when she passed them, stared enviously at the receding feet, and tut-tutted feverishly for the rest of the day; another one wore saucy matelot hats with upturned brims and was heard calling her husband 'Cherub', but that was understandable because she had the misfortune to come from a smart village the other side of Hull; and someone else had a black leather coat probably inspired by Amy Johnson whom everyone had gone to see when she returned from her solo flight to Australia to a triumphant landing at Hedon aerodrome and an ecstatic welcome in Hull. Another pioneering woman, in slacks, who had placed courageous steps along the almost deserted beach at Tunstall – a giant leap for sexual equality — had aroused crocodile tears for her unfortunate daughter who would find it hard to tell the difference between her mother and her father. But war gave all who wanted, the perfect excuse for abandoning skirts for trousers.

Children without shoes were seen in the big cities almost, I suppose, until the outbreak of war but if there had ever been such visual proof of deprivation in Hedon it had disappeared before I was old enough to notice. There were children whose clothes were an indication of poverty even to five-year-olds, and with the cruelty which adults have learnt to camouflage we had no inhibitions about pointing or laughing in the playground at second- and third-hand dresses which had been unsuccessfully cut down and at long trousers roughly shortened and precariously supported by braces fastened to only half the number of buttons intended. Boots, not shoes, were usual for boys, except for Sundays and special occasions, but children and mothers from the poorest homes often wore cheap plimsolls – known as sand shoes – in all weathers, a social stigma now completely eradicated by the classless popularity of scruffy trainers. There was one morning when a little girl arrived at the infants school and told us that her father had been to the police station 'because we have no money', a situation we found incomprehensible but, regrettably, funny. And in the early years of the war when a Christmas party was arranged for much older boys who had performed some public service one or two were seen arriving with sacks over their heads and shoulders as protection against the heavy rain.

A bus journey to Hull made you aware that there were more terrible and frightening things in the world beyond Hedon. Women who looked extremely old in dark dresses and with black shawls shuffled awkwardly from the side streets along Hedon Road to their corner shops. I have read that wives put on their husbands' flat caps back to front to ensure a degree of decorum when they made a brief excursion outside the house, but I never saw anyone wearing such androgynous headgear.

Marks and Spencer were soon to bring about a social revolution and brighten up the streets when they made attractive, colourful clothes an everyday possibility for almost everyone, but in the early post-war years they had still to begin their upwardly mobile progress, and in the Fifties I remember some secretarial students squabbling on a bus because one had accused another of having her clothes bought by her mother at Marks and Spencer's, an insult which was soon to be transformed into a compliment.

The years of liberation came earlier to women than to men, whose innate need to strut as magnificently as peacocks was still deeply submerged beneath Victorian values. Suits had waistcoats, and only dark, or at most, neutral, shades were acceptable, faint stripes were all that was permitted to relieve the monotony of a shirt (though white was preferred), and a dangerous note of nonconformity was struck by a sports jacket or a diamond-patterned pullover or socks.

Clothes are outward and visible signs of attitudes and emotions too private to be articulated, and Hedon people, like everyone else, would eventually be able to dress as they wished and to send out signals conveying messages which had been concealed too long.

My grandfather, Alfred Edwin Markham, enjoyed being an amateur impresario and here he is photographed with his troupe of dancing girls on the sunken lawn of Lambert House.

Entertainment

'Concert' in Hedon meant a variety show: nothing remotely symphonic. Wartime fund-raising weeks and government-inspired holidays at home and other events to keep up morale resulted in a succession of amateur shows, and a poster in a shop window announcing a concert was always scrutinised in happy anticipation.

Sometimes performers came from Hull, usually the pupils of a female impresario who ran an academy of dancing and singing and took her trained troupes on tour through the district as an incentive for them to practise and as an advertisement of her teaching expertise. They were often highly talented and, even if in retrospect they seem glittering and schmaltzy, we were completely uncynical and enjoyed every minute. One semi-professional who brought along her star students was a large lady who led an accordion band. Like most artistes, they performed on the modest stage of the Assembly Rooms, a building with none of the facilities needed for a show, and the concert began to the sound of music vigorously propelled from accordions played invisibly behind the curtains while officials ran from side to side uselessly searching for cords to pull and finally resorting to hefty tugs at the material.

Hedon had a lively group of people interested in amateur dramatics and always ready to put on a show. Harold Cox, a teacher at the school, was a leading light, Stan Register was a popular and practised compère, and Kath Moody and her husband, Arthur, usually game for a song. If there was any self-consciousness it was well hidden, and audiences were far more respectful and appreciative than they later became. The wireless was, I think, a great influence on these amateur performers, who tried to imitate the style of popular comedians and sing like their favourite singers. *We'll gather lilacs in the spring again* had a special significance for people who longed for the end of the war and a chance to lead a normal life. The romantic words and melodies of Ivor Novello were therapeutic music to the ears of listeners who dreamed of a gentler world than the one in which they had too long been condemned to live.

The war finally ended, but in an anti-climatic, unsatisfying way, and memories of a wonderful world before everything changed have never been stronger or more necessary than today. Holderness people who look back to the early years of the century do not forget the hardships, the long hours of tiring manual work and the chronic shortage of cash. But their most vivid memories are usually of the happiness: the occasional treats which were long anticipated and never forgotten, and the colourful characters who set everyone in the village laughing. Television has brought the world into our homes but it has cut us off from our neighbours.

It is easy to romanticise the past, but a lot of pleasure was generated by casual everyday contacts and by informal get-togethers. When few people had cars, travelling into Hull by bus or train was a friendly community activity, and congregations leaving church or chapel would gather in chattering groups to exchange the latest local news.

'We had to make our own entertainment,' is the refrain that comes so often from the lips of those who remember Holderness before the First World War, and the newspapers of the time provide impressive evidence of the energy and effort poured into amateur entertainment and the intense pleasure produced by a village concert. Some events were amazingly ambitious. In January, 1909, a cantata, *Alice in Wonderland,* was performed in Easington on two evenings, obviously by popular demand for, as the *Hull Daily Mail* reported, 'The Easington concerts are famed throughout the neighbourhood.' Audiences were prepared to turn out on dark, cold winter nights, often travelling miles from outlying farms in their eagerness for entertainment which did not come with an effortless flick of a switch. That same month the Hollym dramatic society also put on two evenings of entertainment, and in Withernsea the pupils of Miss Shaw's school of music performed the opera, *Sherwood,* which had 'been in preparation for months'.

Amateur performers in pre-television times had no fear of invidious comparisons with professional artistes and were ready to get up on stage and do their party pieces. In 1906, for example, the teachers and scholars of Aldbrough School gave a concert, again on two evenings, 'to raise funds for the purchase of a school pianoforte'. Every item on the programme was lovingly listed in the press. Hilda Scrowston and Ethel Barker were 'charming' in their rendition of *Pretty Maidens* and *The Cotton Pickers,* great hilarity was roused by 'a most amusing ditty' entitled *The Three Jolly Barbers,* and probably even more by *The Trials of a Schoolmistress,* 'a humorous sketch'.

Boredom was not a problem, and Holderness people of an earlier generation had remarkable stamina. Accustomed to a school discipline which involved a lot of sitting and listening in silence, they could find pleasure in lengthy talks and sermons which now would result in instant yawns and glazed eyes. The great world outside Holderness was largely unknown territory, and, when the Rector of

Roos returned from a visit to the Holy Land, Egypt and Greece, he treated his parishioners to a talk, 'illustrated by a large number of lantern slides, some of which were taken by the lecturer'. Reading was always popular and books were treasured and re-read (often aloud) until their contents were almost known by heart. Branches of the County Library and mobile libraries were for the future, but progress was being made. Easington appears to have been a particularly go-ahead village. In addition to the famed concerts, it was reported that the trustees of Miss Richmond's Free Library had given £5 'towards the establishing of a free library in the parish'. Cards, too, provided easy entertainment both in the home and outside, and on at least one occasion Hedon whist players journeyed out to Ottringham for a match and returned victorious.

Christmas created far more pleasure when it lasted for a couple of days, rather than a week or even a fortnight. It was a season when the better-off were expected to share their good fortune with the less privileged. Though these public displays of philanthropy would not be acceptable in a more egalitarian society, no doubt at the time both donor and recipient derived pleasure from the giving.

Edwardian newspapers maintained the practice of solemnly recording the semi-feudal occasions which the Victorians had regarded as examples of moral conduct deserving public praise: when, for example, Mr. G. Burnham of Burstwick and Master A. Stickney of Ridgmont presented each of their labourers with 'a nice joint of beef for Christmas dinner', when Mrs. Manfield Harrison gave the old women of Burstwick tea and spices, when Mr. W. Baxter presented each widow in Burton Pidsea with five shillings and two stone of flour, and when every poor person in Paull received a bag of coal and two stone of flour from Messrs. Richardson of Little Humber, and another bag of coal from Abraham Leonard. Seasonal merriment could get out of hand and the Edwardian official in Hedon who suffered the indignity of being rolled in the snow when he intervened to stop snowballing may not have thought that he was living in a golden age of innocent self-made entertainment. He would, though, be in a small minority. For most, the happiness still shines brightly.

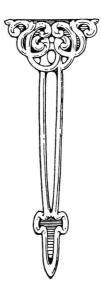

Hull Corporation Bus No. 49 served Hedon during and after the war. The fare for an adult was 10d return, 6d single, and for children 5d return, 3d single.

Going to Hull

Hedon seemed a long way from Hull and a bus journey took you from a familiar world into a place where you kept close to the grown-up who guarded you and waited a long time until it was safe to cross a street. The distance was just over five miles but countryside separated Hedon from Hull, or at least from Marfleet, a village which held on to its own identity and had barely begun its creeping deterioration into a depressing industrial suburb.

Long before the opening of the direct Hedon – Hull road, pedestrians saved three miles by taking a short cut alongside the Humber, probably an uneven grassy path, as the *Hull Advertiser* reported in 1817 that Rev. John Tickell, the distinguished historian, had fallen and fractured his leg while walking from Hedon to Hull 'along the bank'. And long after the road was opened there was nothing remarkable about putting your best foot forward and taking what another Hedon cleric, Rev. Robert Tate, the Catholic priest, described in 1851 as 'a good walk on the gravel causeway all the journey and as level as my parlour floor'.

There were fields all the way to Marfleet and Salt End, and the modernistic Cod Liver Oil factory and the cranes and silo of King George Dock in the distance were just interesting landmarks which aroused no fear that the apartheid which separated Hedon from Hull would soon begin to crumble.

Two pioneering bus services which at different times ran between Hedon and Hull in the years after the First World War had been cheerfully amateurish according to anecdotes passed down. The driver (or maybe conductor) of one would allow his friends to travel free, and the proprietor of the other would treat his passengers to drinks when they arrived at the Hull terminus, two agreeable practices hardly likely to lead to business success.

But *laisser-faire* had been replaced by an efficient Hull Corporation 49 bus when I was taken for my first shadowly remembered ride to Hull. The fare, though, is unforgettable as it remained uninflated long into the post-war years when I travelled daily to school in Hull: 5d return for a child and 10d for an adult, both better buys than single tickets at a punitive 3d and 6d. There was eventually that no-man's-land of one's early teens when trusting conductors would allow you to pay an illegal half fare and adrenalin coursed furiously through your veins until the transaction was safely negotiated. The possibility that a less gullible inspector would board the bus meant that the few pence saved were a hard-earned reward for the agony endured.

During the war it was conductresses only, and it seemed strange when men returned to take over a job which women had been doing perfectly well. I travelled only once on a wartime bus in the dark: it was a macabre experience in an eerie, subdued light, with the conductress carrying a flashlamp and edging her way through passengers standing in the aisle. It was probably cold, as all winter journeys were, by bus or by car, until well after the war, when

Hedon Station. Opened in 1854 on the Hull-Withernsea line, it was one of Dr. Beeching's first casualties in 1964. Built on the town boundary so that the goods yard was outside Hedon and avoided tolls, it was in an inconvenient place for many people.

heating was introduced, first as a luxury and gradually as a necessity. A friend of the same age from another part of Yorkshire agrees with me that one's strongest impression of the late Forties and Fifties is of darkness and cold.

Almost everyone used public transport. Petrol shortages and rationing forced the few privileged people with cars to lay them up 'for the duration', and the passengers on the bus to Hull were as comprehensive a cross-section of the community as a statistician could ever hope to assemble. It was totally democratic, with no class divisions, and the regulars were like members of a club setting out together on a shared adventure, noticing when others were missing, and feeling the group cohesion weaken as the bus neared Hull and people began to leave at stops along the way.

The dark blue and yellow buses of East Yorkshire Motor Services also passed through Hedon, but, even if they were not already full, you were regarded almost like a black-marketeer taking more than your fair share by using a bus intended for someone else when you already had one of your own. It was a more heinous anti-social offence to get on the Withernsea bus in Hull and take the place of someone travelling farther than Hedon who, because of your selfishness, had to be left waving pathetically as the bus passed his stop. It was, in any event, a patriotic duty to stay at home, and inside buses there were posters asking the accusatory question: 'Is your journey really necessary?' As pre-war vehicles became dilapidated, a most painful form of slatted wooden seating was introduced and there was one old bus which carried a plaque proudly recording that it had served in the London Blitz.

After Marfleet traffic noticeably increased. Hedon Road, along with its side streets, was a thickly populated residential area of terraced houses but its importance lay in the docks and related businesses where the people worked. From this unglamorous road Hull derived much of its income and status and, in spite of their traditional hostility, Hedon people were secretly proud to live near what every child knew was Britain's Third Port. Loaded lorries travelled in both directions all day long and a revolution in transport had gathered momentum since a journalist wrote a charming piece in the *Hull Daily Mail* on 17 October, 1929: 'There were no other pedestrians on the broad footpath, and hardly any traffic on the road; a few motor buses were on their way to Hull, and now and then a little motor car would slip quietly by in the opposite direction, and a jogging horse-drawn market cart or two, but otherwise the moon and I had the world to ourselves for most of the way.

'Hedon at night time under a full moon is a quaint old town with its cobbled crooked streets and twisted gables, and on Thursday evening there seemed to be nothing going on except fried fish. I soon found that nearly the whole population had evidently gone to church but the non-churchgoers were as evidently thronging the fish-shops and eating fish.'

The distant location of the railway station on the Preston boundary meant that it was much more usual for us to take the bus, but at one period I went to school in Hull by train. Everyone grumbles about British Rail but the trains of that time were unreliable, slow, uncomfortable — and cold. As steam trains travel further into history they acquire an ever more romantic image, but the filth and grime they produced would horrify a present-day campaigner against pollution, and a winter fog before the Clean Air Acts made a journey by road or by rail a purgatory of slow motion through an almost tangible mass of dirty grey particles.

The Withernsea train left Hull's Paragon Station from its humblest position, Platform One, and the oldest rolling stock was used. Some were museum pieces long pensioned-off until the war recalled them to duty: carriages which now feature in films set in Edwardian England, with sepia photographs of elegant watering places, and luggage racks made,

I think, from artistically knotted cord.

Yet, in spite of all the disadvantages, it was a last opportunity to share, at the end of an era, an experience which had not changed much over a hundred years. There were perfect summer afternoons when the train left Marfleet and travelled with fields on either side until the tower of St. Augustine's came closer into view and Hedon itself seemed encircled by trees in full leaf. Hedon station had its own period charm: a notice that tickets must be 'shewn' and a loop which was acrobatically passed from the engine driver on to the outstretched arm of a porter standing fearlessly on the very edge of the platform for transference to the next train granted access to the stretch of line which remained single-track.

When the first train from Hull to Withernsea arrived in Hedon on 26 June, 1854, there were crowds on the platform, the station was decorated with an arch of evergreen and the church bells rang out in welcome. Thirty years later, Thomas Tindall Wildridge published a handbook for prospective passengers, pointing out the interesting sights they could see *en route* if they peered through their carriage window for there was little to block the view. At Marfleet there was open land as far as the Humber where 'great numbers of sportsmen resort thither from Hull for snipe and seafowl shooting', though the arrival of gangs of navvies working on the new Alexandra Dock had led to a reduction in the bird population. 'Now we bowl on again,' he wrote. 'Looking to the right we see on an elevation about three miles distant the Church of Paull, which appears to hold itself aloof from the village in its care.'

After a potted history of Paull the journey continued for a while. 'Now the train slackens; before it has quite stopped we see out of the window to the left hand a stately tower, rising white from a mass of clustering red brick buildings' — the village of Preston — and then the train arrived at Hedon, 'a fine picturesque old place, it seems; with the memory of its former prosperity hanging over it, like that of a decayed old gentleman who has "seen better days".'

Hedon had much to offer the Victorian tourist, and G. R. Park, the resident historian, had supplied Wildridge with sufficient facts for the most avid passenger to absorb before the engine worked up steam for the next stage of the journey to the coast: 'Farewell, old town, – the train moves on'.

Unfortunately, no more. The halcyon years when Holderness people could visit one of the Hull theatres and take the last train back to Hedon, Withernsea or one of the villages in between now belongs to a remote past, an age of near-perfect public transport, and Nature has taken over the tracks which the Victorians opened up with such zeal and optimism.

Paull Lighthouse, built 1836 by Trinity House but now a private residence, is a landmark for passengers on North Sea Ferries and an unofficial symbol of Holderness.

Paull – Somewhere to Go

Paull was somewhere to go. If you went for a walk or a bike ride you needed a destination and Paull was just far enough to make a journey worthwhile.

We rarely went to Preston, only a mile away compared to Paull's one and a half, but it was not merely a matter of distance. Paull was somewhere different, with a panoramic view of the Humber and of ships sailing between Spurn Point and Hull. There was the tangy smell of salt water, rocks slippery with rubbery seaweed, and a redundant light-house, all giving it as nautical an atmosphere as if it had been on the North Sea coast.

A walk along the winding road to Paull was dull enough to bring a sense of relief when the village was eventually reached. There were plain flat fields on either side, separated from the road by deep ditches and often hidden by high hedges, and only a few landmarks to indicate how far you had gone. First, a searchlight camp, and later its archaeological remains, at a bend in the road; Newton Garth, a large and forbidding red-brick Victorian Gothic farmhouse with an avenue of tall trees darkening the road in front; a bit farther on, New Road, cut through in the early Thirties to shorten the route to Hull; and finally, just before Paull itself, a hutted army camp, abandoned at the end of the war.

A more adventurous way was along a rough footpath of thick grass and overgrown weeds on the raised bank of the Haven until it flowed into the Humber at Paull. It involved passing Salt End, nothing like the extra-terrestrial space station it has since become but already sufficiently large and surrealistic with its complexity of mysterious tanks and pipes and its strange acidic smell which was alien enough to produce a surge of relief when you felt that safety had been reached and you saw the unlovely, welcome mudflats of Paull.

Salt End took its concise, dismissive name from its location on the edge of the Humber and the Haven which made it a stretch of poor quality grassland, liable to flooding with salt water, and so of little commercial value. When Francis Iveson, member of a well-known family of lawyers, was in financial difficulty in the early 19th century he disposed of Salt End, his most expendable bit of property, to raise the few hundred pounds involved – with hindsight, a misjudgement of monumental proportions in view of its future value as a strategically placed industrial site worth a fortune.

Even though you were glad to reach journey's end, the first close-up view of Paull was depressing. The rusting skeletons of clapped-out ships stranded in a riverside breaker's yard were huge and forbidding and an irrational link with the haunting prison hulks in *Great Expectations*. And Paull itself seemed to be a village of dull houses which had lost its vitality and sense of purpose. It had once been a port and later a thriving place where great ships were built for the East India Company and for the Royal Navy during the Napoleonic Wars, but even shrimping, all that was left of its maritime tradition, was now more a leisure-time pursuit than a serious occupation.

For a time, at the turn of the 19th century, when the Georgians were indulging in the new-fangled craze for immersing themselves in cold water, Paull had over-optimistic tourist aspirations, though, in 1793 it had at least one visitor of future celebrity, the

St. Andrew's Church, Paull, not far from the Humber and a casualty from shots fired on the river during the Civil War.

young Tatton Sykes, then a most unlikely banker but already a macho man who walked from Hull to Paull after dinner and bathed in the Humber. In the summer of 1808 Robert Wright, landlord of the Humber Tavern, respectfully informed those who suffered from timidity and inhibitions 'that he has provided a bathing machine, so constructed as to combine convenience with perfect safety and privacy'. Paull, he explained, was pleasantly situated on the Humber and a packet boat sailed three or four times a week between Paull and Hull. One of the added attractions was the opportunity to see a 74-gun ship and a frigate in the course of construction only ten minutes walk from the inn. On 10 November that year H.M. Frigate *Owen Glendower* was launched from Mr. Stevenson's shipyard. Alongside it was the still to be completed *Anson* (named after a man who sailed round the world and was later an M.P. for Hedon), but it was not launched until May, 1811, when it was watched by a crowd which the Hull press originally estimated was between 7 and 8,000, but which was later inflated to 20,000.

That year, 1811, the social amenities of Paull were again on offer when the Grapes, described as a new and substantial inn, was put on the market. It had, as expected, its own bathing machine, and the Grapes was 'in every respect desirable for company who resort there during the Season, the rooms being lofty and pleasant, most of them commanding Humber views'. As a further inducement it was added that the recent establishment of a yard for building men-of-war and merchant vessels was 'daily increasing' property values. Yet – suspiciously — an inn with such potential was for sale, and by the end of the century Paull had a poor reputation as a place frequented by 'low pleasure seekers' who found a wagonette outing to one or more of its pubs much more agreeable than a dip in the Humber and both jollier and cheaper than a train excursion to a seaside resort.

The part of Paull which appeals to me more than

Thorngumbald Clough Lighthouse. The walk from Paull along the Humber bank is highly recommended.

the riverfront is the area round the Church, reached by passing the lighthouse and taking the road which has on its right a strangely shaped building, once the gatehouse to High Paull House, in the 1850s the riverside residence of the thrusting railway entrepreneur, Anthony Bannister, the creator of modern Withernsea, who, as a commuter with style, sailed his own yacht to his office in Hull. The house was demolished c1929 and the site, now a car park, has splendid views of the Humber and is a good starting point for a stroll along the river bank, probably most enjoyable on a summer evening when a North Sea Ferry leaves King George Dock and the water reflects a sky of more subtle beauty as the light begins to fail. Then on the left is a four-square house which has a link with another interesting Victorian character. Paull Manor, now a residential home, was originally the Vicarage, designed by Cuthbert Brodrick, whose surviving masterpieces are the Town Hall and Corn Exchange in Leeds and the Grand Hotel in Scarborough.

Not far along the road is St. Andrew's Church, and the scenery there is to me a microcosm of the English countryside. To the north there are gently undulating fields and in the distance the confident tower of Hedon Church, and to the south, you catch a glimpse of the river. In the Civil War there was nothing tranquil or remote about Holderness. Unlike the Parliamentary stronghold of Hull, Holderness had Royalist sympathies, and the Humber was a lifeline for both sides. The Royalists built a fort at Paull and during a naval skirmish the Church was damaged by stray shots.

The road leads on to Paull Holme tower, all that remains of the moated manor house of the once important Holme family, now regarded by experts as one of the region's most important medieval brick buildings. The tower probably stood at the northern end of the hall, and, like all ruins, it has that mixture of melancholy and romance which lingers round buildings where the glory has departed.

A bit like Paull itself.

Paull Holme, all that remains of a medieval moated manor house.

Inns of Hedon and Holderness

The only inn I knew was the Borough Arms in Havenside. My grandfather had bought it in 1925 to the shock and horror of his wife and daughters who had never before been in a public house and were brought up to regard any woman who entered one as fallen. One day he returned from his weekly visit to his drinking companions in Hull to shock them once more by announcing that, overcome by *bonhomie*, he had sold it to a brewery, though he remained as tenant and was still there, ever on the edge of retirement, in the early years of the war.

I had only occasional glimpses of the public rooms during opening hours when a door was left open, but a rumble that regularly rose and fell and, from time to time, a strident voice that mastered the mêlée penetrated to the living quarters at the rear and the rooms above. On the odd occasions when we were still there at closing time there was the booming voice of my grandfather calling, 'Time, gentlemen, please!'

The demarcation line between the public and private rooms, though, was not always strictly observed. Certain privileged ladies who accompanied their husbands but did not wish to be seen in such circumstances were permitted to sip their whisky, doctored with warm water and a little sugar, by the family fire, and empty orange-coloured beer crates were left in the most inconvenient places, with the sour smell of dregs hovering around them. In the early days a woman had knocked at the back door during the day and asked for old ale. My mother, who was completely innocent in such matters but had seen her father gather up the slops, sold her a bottle of this murky beverage instead of the liqueur-like drink she paid for. There were no complaints.

The Borough Arms had been opened in 1825 as the Corporation Arms, and an incised stone plaque

Proof of ownership: a proud record of the building by the Corporation of the inn now called the Borough Arms.

above the front door recorded the names of the town officials of that time. During the war it had to be camouflaged in case it provided vital information to Nazi invaders unsure of their whereabouts but a coat of whitewash was hardly sufficient to deter the German army.

The inn was some distance from the town centre and, like its predecessor, the Sloop, had been intended as the hostelry for mariners on the Haven nearby, but, although this was an amenity no longer needed, its remote location made it an encouraging objective of a pleasant evening walk and a less prominent drinking place for those not wishing to be labelled as regulars of the town centre pubs.

The tap room had the basic amenities – do I remember spittoons? — and décor which would now make it a mecca for heritage worshippers. But the brewery had restored two other rooms, the smoke room and the lounge, known as the Green Room because of its green wickerwork armchairs and glass-topped tables under which customers slipped cigarette cards which it was impossible to retrieve.

My grandfather was a popular landlord. He was stingy with his family but highly susceptible to flattery and liked to be liked. As a result he was an easy touch for a loan and for drinks on the house and too much of his stock seeped away in free distribution.

The only eatables on sale at the Borough Arms as in most other public houses of that period were crisps and nuts, and we thought it terribly amusing when a stranger called and asked if it was possible to have a sandwich.

As an old market town Hedon was over-provided with inns; and DORA, the long-lasting emergency

Borough Arms, Havenside, formerly the Corporation Arms and bearing a plaque recording its opening in 1825. (During the war it was whitewashed to avoid giving information to invaders.) My maternal grandfather, John Henry Gardner, bought the inn in 1925 and it was from here that my mother was married.

The Shakespeare Inn was formerly the Sir Charles Saunders, named after a distinguished Admiral who served as a Hedon M.P. 1754-1775. When Hedon still had its M.P.s the Sir Charles Saunders was an 'open house' where voters were bribed with food and drink. Travellers from the country 'put up' their vehicles and stabled their horses at the inn.

regulations of the First World War, brought a merciful end to a number which had been in a state of terminal decline for years.

The Rose and Crown, at the crossroads, had become a private house, and the aproned woman who stood at the front door was a Mrs. Simpson who I imagined was a close friend of the Duke of Windsor. A more important inn was the Tiger in the Market Place, then a virtual ruin, which a group of us ran through in terror one afternoon on our way back to school. My next encounter was very much later, after its demolition and replacement by the Post Office, when I was researching Hedon's 19th-century parliamentary elections and realised that it was a popular open house where potential Tory voters were plied with free food and drink.

So too was the Shakespeare when it had its original, more meaningful, name of Sir Charles Saunders, the same as the man who once owned it, a distinguished naval officer and an M.P. for Hedon. Now doing more business than ever in the 1990s and providing meals for which you have to pay but

The Queen's Head, originally the Euryalus but popularly known as the the Horse and Jockey, presumably because the inn sign showed the mythical Euryalus, a mixture of man and horse. Its name was changed to the Queen's Head in 1837 at the accession of Victoria – but the modern inn sign incorrectly shows Elizabeth I.

far distance. The Dog and Duck was Drescher's grocery shop with the original bar converted into a counter, still showing the marks where the pumps had been fixed. This was a business which had its windows broken in a stupid outbreak of chauvinism when, in reprisal for Zeppelin raids, anyone with a German name, like the Dreschers, who had come to England as clockmakers, had to suffer the customary fate of the innocent.

Apart from the Borough Arms, the existing inns of Hedon were merely mysterious places outside which small groups of flush-faced men had noisy and irrational conversations and from which unpleasant people emerged.

Old pubs, since then, have become academically respectable, a popular subject for local historians, and Holderness inns would be a splendid subject for a best-seller. Even if the book never materialised, the research involved would provide an agreeable approach to social history. Quite a number of these names reflect the rural character of Holderness and particularly the use of horse-drawn transport. There's the Plough at Hollym, the White Horse at Easington and Ottringham, the Nag's Head at Burstwick and Preston, the Bay Horse at Arnold, the Blacksmith's Arms at Coniston and Preston, the Coach and Horses at Welwick, and the Black Horse at Atwick and Roos. Burton Pidsea has two animal inns, the Black Bull, and the Nancy which commemorates a famous 19th-century horse which enjoyed a marvellous run of success, and country sports feature in the Hare and Hounds at Burstwick and the Falcon at Withernwick.

There are links with the great families of the area: the Constable Arms at Sproatley, and the Hildyard Arms at Patrington. The Watts Arms, Ottringham, is named after the Lords of the Manor: like the Dacre Arms, Brandesburton (formerly the Cross Keys), after Lady Dacre.

Victorians welcomed the railway and quickly discarded historic names for signs. The opening of the Holderness Railway from Hull to Withernsea in

which must compare favourably with anything provided for corrupt Georgian voters, it still has the large yard where country people, like my grandparents from Little Humber, put up their pony and trap when they caught the train to Hull.

The Greyhound had become Mrs. Marlow's pastry shop, and a hint of its former layout was the series of rooms through which she seemed to travel, along a stone-flagged route from her kitchen in the

1854 turned Hedon's Durham Ox into the more modern Station Hotel, and other places along the line followed suit: Patrington with another Station Hotel and Ottringham with a Railway Hotel. On the Hornsea line, opened ten years later, is New Ellerby's Railway Inn.

Some have deeper historical roots. The Cross Keys at Cowden is the papal symbol, a reminder that some of the earliest hostelries were provided by the Church for travellers and pilgrims, and the George and Dragon both at Aldbrough and Holmpton, honours the patron saint of England. The Crown and Anchor at Elstronwick and Kilnsea sounds as if it comes in this category, but Withernsea's historian, John Whitehead, points out that 'Crown and Anchor' was a popular gambling game in the navy which later spread to troop ships – and presumably took hold in coastal villages.

Easington's Granby commemorates the 18th-century Marquis of Granby, a popular hero, whose hat or wig (versions differ) fell off when he was leading a cavalry charge, causing him to go bald-headed at the enemy (the origin of the phrase), with his men loyally following his gleaming dome like a victory torch. Withernsea no longer has its Raglan, military leader in the Crimean War, but the Alma still commemorates the battle of 1854. More sedately, the resort's Alexandra (1871) recalls the newly-married Princess of Wales, destined to be the long-suffering wife of Edward VII, and Hornsea, too, has its Alexandra.

Apart from the church, an inn was often the only public place in a village before community centres were invented. As well as providing food and drink they were the venue for auctions, for meetings, for local courts and for inquests, and farmers traditionally prefer dealing in convivial surroundings.

Coaches and carriers' carts called to pick up or put down passengers or goods, and town directories published details of services available. A typical directory, published in 1840, advertised 'coaches from Hornsea to Hull daily during the bathing season' and Patrington was exceptionally well endowed with transport facilities. Each Tuesday Wing's Omnibus left at 7 a.m. and the Mail Coach at 8.15 a.m., Wing's coach left on Tuesdays and Fridays at 7 a.m., and carriers left the Hildyard Arms on the same days.

One problem facing historians of hostelries is the – persisting – habit of landlords and breweries of changing names. The Queen's Head at Hedon was formerly the Euryalus, a difficult name for a slurred speaker to pronounce, and, as the mythical half-animal, half-human Euryalus would appear on an inn sign as something like a man on a horse, the likely reason for its being popularly known as the Horse and Jockey. The re-naming as the Queen's Head took place in 1837, the year of Victoria's accession, and surely she, not Elizabeth I, should have her portrait on the modern sign.

Three finely-bound volumes, *The Country Inns*, part of a series, *Holderness, in Picture and Story*, written by Mr. J. Wilson Smith of Hornsea in 1953, are in typescript, available for reference only at the Local Studies Library, Albion Street, Hull. The work has acquired added interest over the past 41 years and is now a period piece, heavy with nostalgia, its black and white photographs capturing for all time the appearance of the inns of Holderness as they were, and as they remained until well after the war.

Change does not necessarily mean decline, and the author's gloomy speculations about the uncertain future of the Shakespeare in Baxtergate have been disproved. 'It would,' he wrote, 'indeed be a loss to the amenities of Hedon if this picturesque old Inn were to close down. But, indeed, it lies in a quiet, little back-water, and there seems little chance of a living here under present commercial conditions.' Baxtergate is now part of a busy one-way system, and there are no empty tables in the Shakespeare at lunch time.

Stanley Wilson — M.P. for Holderness

I lost out on elections because the outbreak of war prolonged the life of the Parliament elected in 1935 for an exceptional ten-year term. The political truce of coalition government stifled controversy, though by-elections in other parts of the country provided opportunities for the frustrated to win seats as Independents, and for a time a new Commonwealth Party had a run of success. Locally, nothing stirred.

The reputation which Hedon had earned as a parliamentary borough which had taken bribery and corruption to new depths of notoriety had plummeted after the 1832 Reform Act removed its two M.P.s. Times had changed since a former M.P., Anthony Browne, an affluent director of the East

Arthur Stanley Wilson, known to his family as 'Jack', the son of Arthur Wilson, the shipping magnate of Tranby Croft, was the young man who played a crucial role in the Baccarat Scandal by revealing the cheating which he claimed to have witnessed when the Prince of Wales was a guest. He served as Conservative M.P. for Holderness from 1900 until 1922.

Stanley Wilson M.P. addressing the crowds after his narrow victory in 1906.

Reproduced from a photograph loaned by Miss G. Morley

India Company, who had been forced to transfer a portion of his wealth into the pockets of avaricious Hedon voters, could sarcastically say of an elector: 'He is a voter of Hedon. I believe he lives entirely upon that circumstance and that circumstance alone.' Yet Hedon loved an election and long after the Reform Act there were elderly residents who mourned the passing of the days when elections were boisterous, colourful carnivals of processions, free food and free drink.

Elections after the Second World War were deadly dour in comparison with those of the past and there were nostalgic memories, no longer of Georgian times, but of the years from 1900 to 1922 when Stanley Wilson was M.P. for Holderness.

He had been the young man at Tranby Croft who claimed to have seen Sir William Gordon Cumming cheating at baccarat in September, 1890, when the Prince of Wales was the guest of his father, the shipping magnate, Arthur. If only he had kept his suspicions to himself he would have strangled at birth a whole army of rumour, innuendo and speculation which refuses to die and which has recently been given a further lease of life by a new play, *The Royal Baccarat Scandal.*

When Stanley Wilson – known in the family as Jack – gave evidence during Gordon Cumming's vain attempt to clear his name in court he sounded more like Bertie Wooster than a future M.P. To the Solicitor General's question, 'What is your occupation?' he replied with a nonchalance not far removed from downright rudeness, 'I don't know that I have any occupation. I don't do much.' And when he was asked why he left Cambridge after only a year he was equally laid-back: 'Because I did not do much work up there and I thought it rather a waste of time.' He had entered Father's business and worked very hard – for just one month.

The comfortably cushioned life-style of a gilded youth was hardly an ideal preparation for a man who was to represent at Westminster the hard-working, level-headed residents of such a large rural constituency as Holderness, but young Stanley appears to have improved with age. He was never more than a run-of-the-mill back-bench M.P. but he attracted a loyal following of supporters who always regarded him with respect and affection. Unlike his Uncle Charles and two cousins who all served as Liberal M.P.s, Stanley was a Conservative, first winning Holderness at an easy election in 1900 when his party benefited from the jingoistic fervour generated by the Boer War. Six years later, when the political pendulum had swung violently against the Tories and the Liberals enjoyed a spectacular landslide, he managed to hang on to what should have been a safe seat by a dangerously narrow majority of 29 votes.

In the early years of the century the enthusiasm for politics was remarkable. Voters were not sated with a never-ending media coverage of election campaigns, children fought their parents' political battles in the playground, party colours were bravely worn and party songs lustily sung, and, after a long working day, people crammed into meetings for a chance to see and hear the men who wanted their votes.

In 1906 a meeting in Hornsea drew in crowds of Wilson supporters, and the *Hull Times* dismissed with contempt any evidence of opposition. 'There were a few Radicals in the usual place at the rear,' it conceded, 'but they appeared very youthful and it is doubtful whether there was a voter amongst them. They were present apparently for fun which they appeared to get out of their irrelevant interruptions of the speakers, and when the proper time came after Mr. Wilson's address not one of them could ask an intelligent question.' Wilson undertook a formidable round of public meetings, and Ottringham, Burstwick, Mappleton and Withernsea all had their turn. A visit to Aldbrough was enlivened by the attendance of several Radicals who, like their friends at Hornsea, were 'on the look-out for sport'. Various speakers had to keep their audience's attention until Wilson arrived at around nine o'clock, delayed by the break-down of his car, and when he eventually appeared he remarked that 'motor cars were queer and unreliable things'. It was a sentiment which assured him the support of at least one old countryman who had no time for these new-fangled contraptions and shouted out his agreement: 'Aye, they all want skellin' up.'

One of Wilson's strongest cards was his membership of an important local family, and his distinguished Liberal opponent in 1906, E. J. Wilberforce, a descendant of the Emancipator, received short-shrift from the Chairman of the Holderness Tories: 'An East Riding man was far better qualified to represent them than was a barrister from the West Riding.' An elderly lady I have spoken to who had made rosettes for Wilson at elections remembered him as a genial man who never wanted to become embroiled in political discussions. He seems, though, to have been a capable constituency M.P. by the standards of the time. And if he did not make his mark as a great parliamentary orator, he was a regular attender and voter in the Commons: in 1906 it was said that he had been through the Division Lobbies on 1,258 occasions. Accompanied by his wife, the former Alice Filmer, he visited Patrington Workhouse and the press duly reported that Mrs. Wilson had left ten shillings to be divided among the women. More significantly, when South Holderness suffered serious flooding following an exceptionally high tide, he raised the problem in the Commons and asked for financial help for the victims. The evasive reply was typical of Government ministers in such situations: 'The question of coast protection is about to be considered by a Royal Commission.'

In 1910, a year of two general elections, there were more strenuous tours of a far-flung constituency which at that time stretched as far as Beverley, and Hornsea, Withernsea, Brandesburton, Sigglesthorne, Keyingham, Thorngumbald, Paull and Hedon were all on Wilson's itinerary. 'At Sunk Island he dealt extensively with the subject of Tariff Reform.'

Stanley Wilson was probably happier as a sportsman than a politician. He was a great racing man and he still found time to ride with the Holderness Hunt during his election campaign in January, 1910. He was successful in all his contests until 1922 when Holderness farmers, sensing that he 'had not maintained his previous touch with agriculture', withdrew their support.

Defeat brought his parliamentary career to an end. He had not achieved the success of Uncle Charles who had been granted a peerage and the sonorous title of Lord Nunburnholme, but he was not a man to let misfortune dent his customary cheerfulness. He had, in fact, 16 years of happy retirement before his death in 1938, when an obituary recorded: 'His hearty laugh was as familiar on the course as it was in the House of Commons.'

Many modern politicians would welcome such an uncritical comment on their parliamentary careers.

Harrowing in the 1930s. Horses were often used on farms in the Second World War.

The lonely landscape of Little Humber.

The long daily journey from Little Humber to school, often in the dark and in bad weather, made the first glimpse of home a welcome sight for my mother and her brothers and sisters.

Little Humber — *Back of Beyond*

Little Humber was very familiar to me long before I ever visited it.

My mother was born there in 1903, one of the eight children of the farm foreman who had taken up the job when he was newly married and who stayed on until Martinmas, 1925. Childhood is the most important part of our lives and my mother's deepest memories, which I loved to hear, were of the years she lived at Little Humber.

Nothing had made a stronger impact on her than the isolation of the family home, not far from the Humber bank and miles from a village. The only other house nearby belonged to the farmer, and a journey to Thorngumbald or Paull was a major undertaking, often, too, a test of stamina. A day in Hull was a rare event. The tiring journey began with a ride in a horse-drawn vehicle to Hedon to join the train from Withernsea and usually ended with everyone returning with a headache brought on by the noise and chaos of city streets. Long before the day was over my grandmother would be crippled, for there were times when she would never leave the house for weeks and she was unaccustomed to outdoor shoes and walking on hard pavements.

There were, of course, no school buses, and travelling to Thorngumbald School in a donkey cart along roads cruelly exposed to the winds and rain of Holderness was an appalling ordeal for young children to undergo, often in the dark during winter months. It was made worse by the horrors awaiting them at school, for the harsh discipline and the sarcasm of the master was a traumatic experience which remained with her for the rest of her life. These were only children of primary school age and yet on dark afternoons the master would make a show of lighting lamps in the classroom and stressing how late he would make them stay, while they cringed, dreading the long, cold ride ahead of them before they reached the safety of home.

But, in spite of the isolation and the hardship, it was far from being a time of unending misery. Children are resilient, and there were enough of them in the family to create their own amusement. There was no television, but intense pleasure was provided by such events as a harvest festival, an amateur concert or, as they grew older, a dance in the Institute at Thorngumbald, all anticipated with keen excitement and looked back upon with undimmed joy.

Fortunately these and many other memories will not be lost, for a few years ago I persuaded my mother to write her reminiscences and these were published under the title, *Back of Beyond*, a book which brought her a lot of pleasure as she received letters from people all over the world whose memories coincided with hers.

Back of Beyond had to be reprinted but is currently out of print. Until I needed to check some details I had not opened it for quite some time and I was delighted to realise how well it read and how vividly it re-created life in Holderness in the early years of the century. One of my favourite passages selected by the local author, Bruce Crowther, for inclusion in an anthology he has edited, *A Celebration of Yorkshire*, conveys the authentic atmosphere of Little Humber: 'Although it could be bleak and lonely, as children we had many happy times on the banks of the river, and it is an area for which I have great feeling. One of the nicest sounds I remember was going to the Humber after the tide had been up and hearing the river banks all settling again, little pools of water running here and there and the sea-birds calling out as they found anything and everything the tide had left behind. The smell was one I never forget — fresh salty air and a beautiful smell from tufts of small flowers whose name I think was Thrift. I feel I can still hear the gurgling of the water finding its way over the mud flats.'

Although Little Humber was so remote, it has its place in the history of England. Originally part of the estate of Earl Tostig, who was slain at the Battle of Stamford Bridge in 1066, it was granted after the Norman Conquest to the Counts of Aûmale (Albemarle), the Lords of Holderness, but by the 13th century was under the direct administration of the Crown. When Wyke and Myton (the nucleus of Kingston upon Hull) were acquired by Edward I from Meaux Abbey, the monks received Little Humber as part of the deal.

It was an area of meadows and pastures, increasing in size as land was reclaimed and losing many acres in times of heavy flooding. To oversee this outlying property a grange (probably a moated house) was established there and by 1749 a farm known as Old Little Humber occupied the site. A new Little Humber, the farm where my mother eventually lived, had come into existence, and a lane giving access to it was cut through the fields.

By the 16th century Little Humber belonged to the Constables of Burton Constable and in the 19th century the 400-acre farm was rented by successive generations of Richardsons, well-known farmers in that part of South Holderness. Thomas was there in the 1840s and '50s; then came William, Joseph and Lewis, followed by another William who appears to have taken over around the time my grandfather moved to Little Humber, still only 22, but a young man of ability and self-confidence.

Mr. Richardson obviously shared this confidence and told him that his job was not to work himself, but to see that the men worked hard. It was a responsibility he took very seriously, too seriously at times and he made himself unpopular by his dictatorial methods and his erratic outbursts of temper. The men (hired annually) slept in a room in his house known as the Chamber, addressed him as 'Maister', and took their meals under his watchful eye. There were two tables in the kitchen and my grandmother and the children sat at one, while my grandfather took his place at the head of the men's table, carving and dishing out their food. Meals were straightforward and predictable, but both quality and quantity were excellent for my grandmother and the girls were all skilful cooks. Courses were, however, served in reverse order, suet pudding coming first so that hearty appetites would be dulled before the meat appeared.

Little Humber was part of the parish of Paull and a journey to thee church or village involved passing along an eerie stretch of road where the overhanging trees formed an arch with their topmost branches. It was known as Dark Lane and my mother was always glad to emerge into the light at the other end.

She finished her memoirs with a verse which showed that she was prepared to accept the bad as well as the good in those years at Little Humber:

> 'Now I have re-lived my twenty-one years,
> There have been laughter, shadow and tears,
> But, given the chance to live it again,
> I would go once more down memory's Bright Lane.'

That is what local history is about: looking back, not with anger or sentimentality, but with joy and thankfulness.

Home Cooking

I recently bought something calling itself a Yorkshire curd cheese-cake. It was – well – all right, but nothing like the ones my mother used to make. She needed no recipe book but followed, almost by instinct, the traditional method she had picked up from her mother in a Holderness kitchen and which had probably been handed down through many generations. In spite of the lack of written instructions the results were superb: a rich, luscious filling made even better by a generous scattering of well-soaked currants, and, best of all, a gooey layer where the moisture had begun to seep into the pastry.

'Yorkshire' tagged on to the name of a modern dish suggests quality, but the reality often falls short of the promise. Yorkshire Pudding appears on menus all over Britain but most of them should be arrested as imposters. A real Yorkshire pudding is beautifully smooth, melts in the mouth, and is far too good to be a mere adjunct to a meal, fully deserving its place of honour as a course in its own right. In some eating establishments the emphasis is on

The Albert Kitchener Range was typical of the cooking and heating system of many houses well into the mid-20th century. Until the coming of gas, the fire had to be lit before a kettle could be boiled and food cooked for breakfast.

quantity rather than quality, and the end product is a mound of flabby substance edged with a crust resembling burnt biscuit.

A new interest in regional food has led to more shops selling goods of home-made quality and there are probably more good cooks around than there were even ten years ago, but earlier in the century almost every Holderness home had its regular baking day when pantries were stocked with competition-standard pies and cakes for the following week. Electric and gas cookers need no laborious stoking, and marathon baking sessions are as outdated as dreaded washdays, but many are convinced that modern methods (particularly of cultivation) produce food that has lost its taste. Elderly Holderness residents become lyrical as they reminisce about deep custard pies, and mouth-watering apple pies not made of bland, anonymous apples, eaten with chunks of cheese that had never been out of England. They remember bramble 'cakes' (pies which had the bottom layer of pastry overlapping the top to keep in the juice) and currant 'cakes' which merited a government health warning, packed with fruit, recklessly sweetened and, for good measure, covered with a sugary glaze.

Tea is the meal at which Yorkshire excels: not a cup of tea and a biscuit but a kitchen table laden with pork pie, ham and egg cake, sausage rolls, ham, rich fruit loaf, a bewildering selection of pastry and cakes, and all the chutneys, pickles, jams and custard you might fancy to add that finishing touch. This is the way Yorkshire maintains a traditional style of feasting which goes back at least to medieval times when, instead of a sequence of separate courses, an array of dishes was spread before the guests.

Holderness people like a substantial tea, but for farming folk the main meal, eaten at midday, was

Ladies doing-good in a soup kitchen. Before the coming of the Welfare State such charity was vital in times of unemployment.

always called dinner. Nowadays it is more customary, especially for those who work away from home, to have dinner in the evening but I think it odd when hotels offer a sumptuous midday meal on 25 December and call it 'Christmas lunch'. Are they really suggesting that this is a mere prelude to something even grander in the evening?

Men who had spent a long morning tramping behind a pair of heavy horses dragging a plough through Holderness clay would have looked in disbelief if they had been offered an artistically arranged 'ploughman's lunch'. The word, 'lunch', was used to describe the hefty snacks carried in baskets to men working in the fields at haymaking and harvest as their ''lowance' to keep them going unttil they broke off for a proper meal, Paper-thin, almost transparent, slices of meat sold in delicatessens have no resemblance to the strong, salty wedges cut from a shoulder of home-cured ham that hung from a ceiling hook. The ritual of pig-killing had a renaissance during the war when it became the obvious, if not always legal, way of supplementing miniscule rations, and provided a cornucopia of sausages and unpleasant looking but exceedingly tasty bits and pieces described, unflatteringly, as offal. The quantity of food for instant consumption was more than most households could consume, and, when the fatted pig was killed, friends and neighbours were given a 'fry' in the firm expectation that they would return the favour when plenty reigned in their houses.

Long before cholesterol hit the headlines, it was an article of faith that fat was good for you, and children were reprimanded if they left any fat on their plates. Much harder living and working conditions meant that a high intake of calories did not necessarily result in a weight problem, and disobeying modern health advice certainly produced one celebrated local man who was thin and wiry and lived to a great age. The fame of Sir Tatton Sykes spread from the Wolds into Holderness where the family owned much land, and both his grandfather, Mark, and his brother, Christopher, were Rectors of Roos. Sir Tatton did not breakfast on muesli but on a bowl of new milk, fruit tart, lumps of fat, stout and cream. He lived to be nearly 91, and was breaking stones a few days before his death.

Even in the post-war years I remember the disgust expressed by a group of Holderness housewives about a neighbour who actually *bought* her bread, a practice they regarded as a sure sign of decadence. Tins of dough, lined up on the hearth to 'rise', were an everyday sight, and fresh warm baking-powder cakes, cut in half and spread with golden syrup (usually called treacle), were — I hope still are — one of life's purest pleasures. Connoisseurs of good food in Holderness have access to one delicacy not much known in other parts of the country – rock semper (or samphire) which grows on the Humber bank and is sometimes known as poor man's asparagus: it's cheaper than the real thing but hardly inferior.

Proust was inspired to write a masterpiece of French literature by the taste of a cake which brought memories of childhood flooding back. Maybe one day a real Yorkshire 'crud' cheesecake will have a similar effect on an English writer.

Holderness Talk

A break-down in Anglo-American relations resulted when a number of us on a coach tour passed a leaflet round so that everyone could have a 'skeg'. In the group was an American lady whose husband has a post at BP Chemicals, Salt End. 'Skeg' mystified her. She had never before encountered this concise Holderness word for 'a quick look' and she wrote it down, presumably to mystify other Americans when she returns to the United States.

Buildings are a link with the past but words take us into the very minds of our ancestors and bring into focus a way of life that was lived close to the land, when the seasons and the weather were all-important. Holderness dialect carries the imprint of the early settlers who came to this coastal region from northern Europe, and many village names and much local vocabulary have their roots in the languages spoken by Anglo-Saxon and Viking invaders. As people move away from their rural past it is hardly surprising if dialect declines, and I am fascinated by the contents of a book published in 1877, *A Glossary of Words used in Holderness*, by Frederick Ross, Richard Stead and (appropriately) Thomas Holderness. It brings back memories of childhood and reminds me of people and events I had forgotten and of words I had never heard for years. Americans speak of autumn as 'fall' but Holderness has the more emotive 'back-end' of the year. 'Caud' conveys the rigours of our raw climate far more forcefully than the conventional 'cold'; 'rooak' is as mournful as the mist creeping in from the North Sea; and no one who has trudged wearily through the 'blather' of a muddy lane could ever find a better word than 'clarty' to describe the state of his 'beeyats'.

Holderness expressions have a strength, a vigour and a directness which make them a welcome contrast to the verbiage uttered by politicians and public figures who often use words to conceal meaning. People whose labours provided

Holderness pronunciation can cause problems of communication, as a school inspector found when he asked a pupil her mother's name.

little more than their basic needs had no time for fancy phrases. 'Gawmless' was the bluntest condemnation of anyone who failed to use commonsense, and 'tonnup-heed' would not now be considered politically correct but it left no doubt about its meaning. 'Whitherty-whitherty' is a wonderful way of describing a state of indecision, and in an unheated bedroom on a cold winter night you certainly need to 'hap' yourself up with 'happin'.

Dialect is essentially a spoken language which loses its colour when you attempt to translate it into print. Sam Weller's Cockney conversation is a pain to a solitary reader but it springs into life in the mouth of a talented actor. In the same way, you have to hear a Holderness housewife say 'wesh' to realise it's a far more strenuous job than a simple 'wash', just as there's a world of difference between conventional 'black' and the 'bleck' that describes the coagulated grease or oil of a cart or machine. Holderness children probably continue to 'worrit' their parents, kicking up a 'racket' with their 'bealin', and parents may respond by 'chowing' at their recalcitrant offspring, either promising a 'good skelpin' or threatening: 'Ah'll gie thee bell-tinker!'

Nearness to nature involved regular contact with birds and animals, and many were given local names. 'Cuddie' is still the fairly common name for a hedge sparrow, a 'bare-golly' is an unflattering description of a featherless bird; a 'banty cock' refers to a strutting, conceited person as well as a bantam-cock itself. Even less frequently heard today is 'pricky (or prickly) back otshin' for 'hedgehog' – the 'otshin' being the Holderness version of the Old English 'urchin'.

A local mannerism is converting 't' into 'th' so that 'treacle' becomes 'threacle'. A difficult question was raised by an elderly farmer a few years ago when an intruder broke into the Queen's bedroom. Accustomed to male superiority, the old man asked in genuine amazement, 'But weer was Maisther?' That really happened but I am not certain about the story of the motorist who was used to the local substitution of 'while' for 'until' and caused an accident when he misinterpreted a notice, 'Wait while the signal is at red'.

The local pronunciation of 'curd' is 'crud', and there are a number of Holderness sayings which confuse people from other parts of the country. Here we 'mash' tea, eat, not 'loaves of bread', but 'bread-loaves', and we 'mend' fires. 'Cabbish' is 'cabbage', and no one ever invented a more appropriate word for describing a depressing day or a depressed person than 'dowly': the very sound echoes with melancholy. I have heard of 'going Dutch' but the old glossary of Holderness words says that 'going Yorkshire' had the same meaning, an indication of the 'nearness' of folk who didn't 'chuck their brass around' and, even if they were well-off and had made 'a bonny penny', merely admitted that they were 'comfortable'.

Those unfortunate enough to live on the other side of the Humber were contemptuously dismissed as 'Lincolnshire Yalla Bellies', apparently from the yellow-bellied frogs that abounded there. If the County of Humberside is abolished and Lincolnshire goes its separate way, no doubt we shall hear that customary Holderness farewell: 'Good shutness to bad rubbish!'

St. German's Church, Winestead, a small, unspoilt village church but with an atmosphere of quiet elegance. On Winifred Holtby's map of 'South Riding' the fictional 'Maythorpe' coincides with Winestead. Andrew Marvell, the poet, was baptised here in 1626.

Holderness Churches

Hilston Church, for me at least, is a symbol of Holderness.

It may seem strange that from an area of outstanding medieval churches I should select for this starring role a modern building of uncharacteristic appearance with its Scandinavian-style tower. But I remember as a child returning from Tunstall with my parents and stopping at the ruins of the earlier church on the site, built in 1861 and devastated on 18 August 1941 by a bomb dropped by a German plane which, after raiding Hull, had apparently released its remaining cargo on the last prominent building in view before leaving land. I can't remember the date of our visit (it must have been some years later – surely we would not be on the beach in 1941 ?), but I know that we got out of the car and walked among jagged lumps of masonry scattered all around.

The present church, the third on the site, was not re-built until 1957, and during the long years of waiting Hilston people worshipped in a house. It was a building worth waiting for, with its light, tranquil, uncluttered interior and a supremely beautiful east window, subtle variations on a theme, in blue stained glass. Some things were rescued from the ruined church and incorporated into the

St. Patrick's Church, Patrington, the Queen of Holderness and the graceful consort of Hedon's King. Highly praised by John Betjeman, who wrote: 'The stateliest Decorated parish church, within and without, that I know is at Patrington. It sails in honey-coloured limestone like a ship over the flat estuary land at the mouth of the Humber.'

Holy Sacrament Catholic Church, Marton. Church and priest's house were constructed as one unit so that the religious nature of the building was camouflaged in less tolerant times.

new building, among them pieces of a window erected in memory of Rev. Christopher Sykes, brother of the legendary Sir Tatton. Even more remarkably, you still enter through the Norman doorway with its typical zig-zag decoration which was originally installed in Hilston's first church and has stood firm through all the changing scenes of life, defying Victorian restoration and Hitler's bombs.

This is why I regard St. Margaret's, Hilston, as a symbol of Holderness. Two parallel strands, continuity and change, run through so much of its history. This is an area whose roots go deep into the past, and yet it has renewed its strength with each generation by adapting, where necessary – like Hilston church, taking on a new appearance but preserving the link with its earliest days.

Old buildings were once brand new, and churches now regarded as a traditional part of the Holderness landscape probably startled local people by their novel design when they were first built. None more so than St. Augustine's at Skirlaugh, donated to the village in 1401 by its 'local boy made good', Walter de Skirlaw (or Skirlaugh), successively Bishop of Lichfield, Wells and Durham. Such a powerful and wealthy benefactor had the means to create a work of art on the grandest scale in the new Perpendicular style, the prototype of what was eventually to become a feature of so many churches in the neighbourhood. Small things have a habit of providing just as much pleasure as those designed to be admired, and one of the particular delights of Skirlaugh Church is the graffiti, a number of signatures, probably carved by

St. Mary's Church, Welwick, another genuine village church, still with evidence of the 19th-century school at the west end of the nave. My maternal grandmother was brought up in this village by an uncle and aunt and she remembered him wearing a top hat for church.

soldiers stationed there during the Civil War.

Skirlaugh Church was built in one piece as a unified structure, but another village church, St. German, Winestead, is an undramatic but impressive example of the typical Holderness story – the adaptation and alteration of a building over the centuries in accordance with changing taste and needs. Winestead's original 12th-century church was enlarged 200 years later. There were more alterations in the 15th century, with new windows installed and the nave re-built. The Hildyard Chapel was added in the 17th century and the men who fitted a new north door conveniently carved the date on it – 1694. In the late 19th century there was a formidable restoration and a new porch built in 1901. Miraculously, the medley of items and styles passed down over many centuries fuses into an integrated whole, not a museum piece but a building that has always been a living part of the village.

St. Mary's at Welwick is another with the feel of a real village church. Some churches have been over-restored and their vitality has been damaged, but here you can see how the building has grown over the years to suit the needs and aspirations of succeeding generations. Welwick Church has what the distinguished local historian, Mr. K. A. MacMahon, used to call 'churchwardens' restoration': the extra lancet inserted into a window in the south wall of the chancel, a practical way of providing more light for the officiating priest, and a bit of medieval do-it-yourself making you more aware of Welwick people of long ago than something grand. Another example of village workmanship is the tomb probably brought from the lost Priory of Burstall and inserted, less than perfectly, into the south wall of the nave. But the feature which intrigues me most of all is the door leading into the area at the west end which served as the village school into the 19th century. Everyone knows that early schools had a close connection with the Church, but at Welwick theory is transformed into reality. This is what a church school was really like.

Quite different in atmosphere and style is the little Catholic church at Marton, easy too to miss because it was deliberately built in 1789 to be

St. Augustine's Church, Skirlaugh, a perfect example of Perpendicular architecture, donated to the village by the locally born Bishop Walter de Skirlaw.

unobtrusive. It stands in a secluded position well off the road and could easily be mistaken for a Georgian farmhouse: it is plain, rectangular, and built of brick, and merges into what was originally the priest's residence attached to its side. A discreet domestic style enabled a Catholic church to be erected before legal discrimination was finally ended. Its interior is quiet and subdued, as unostentatious as it appears from outside.

The King and Queen of Holderness are famous far beyond the county boundary but to ignore them because they are well-known would be an unforgivable act of *lèse-majesté*. Patrington, the Queen, occupies a high place in the first division of churches throughout the country, not merely in Holderness, and Nikolaus Pevsner, who inspected almost every building worth seeing in England, came to that very conclusion. 'For sheer architectural beauty,' he wrote, 'few parish churches in England can vie with Patrington.' Another enthusiast was John Betjeman who considered it 'the stateliest Decorated parish church', both inside and out, he had ever encountered. Being a poet, he could sing its praises in memorable words: 'It sails in honey-coloured limestone like a ship over the flat estuary land at the mouth of the Humber.'

Its regal consort, St. Augustine's at Hedon, is a more masculine building and its forthright tower is a perfect complement to the graceful spire of Patrington, both prominent landmarks in the Plain of Holderness. Hedon is more a civic church, its history inextricably intertwined with that of the town, and has a cushion for its splendid mace to rest upon when the Mayor is in attendance. For me, once again, it is the minor items which stay longest in the memory: the elegant 18th-century memorial to the benefactress, Ann Watson, the far plainer one to John Tickell, the early historian of Hull, who lived in Fletchergate, and the photographs in the vestry of former vicars.

The late Charles Dann, a long-serving vicar and one of the great characters of Holderness, used to tell a nice story against himself. On one occasion, when the Archbishop of York was robing before a service, Mr. Dann, taking advantage of the opportunity, drew his attention to the pictures. 'You will notice, Your Grace,' he said, 'that two of my predecessors became bishops — and there is space for a third.' He would chuckle as he admitted that the Archbishop had failed to take the hint.

His elevation to the episcopal bench would have been a gain for Their Lordships but a loss to Hedon and Holderness.

St. Margaret's Church, Hilston. Built 1957 to replace the Victorian church, bombed in 1941, it still retains the Norman doorway from the first church on the site: a remarkable example of change and continuity.

Burton Constable Hall, the one stately home in Holderness, built in the 16th century but much altered in the 18th century.

Burton Constable Hall

My first visit to Burton Constable Hall was years before it opened regularly to the paying public. Alfie Birtles, the much ridiculed but highly influential history master at Hymers College, had written for permission to take his Field Club and we went by coach one Wednesday afternoon.

We were welcomed at the front of the house by Brigadier Raleigh Chichester Constable whom Mr. Birtles always addressed by his title, and, before we trooped inside, the Brigadier, with that studied dismissiveness I have since seen adopted by most stately home-owners when they refer to the enormity of their possessions, explained how he had enlarged his front lawn simply by moving back the fence separating it from the park, the easiest way to make a larger lawn in his opinion. It was meant to be amusing and there was an obedient titter. I probably joined in but I thought it a vulgar remark.

It was my first visit to a stately home and I was overwhelmed, though not excited, by the experience. The house was enormous but it was dead, drab and depressing and the only thing I particularly remember was the Chinese Chippendale which stuck in my memory because of its incongruity and its alliteration.

The Brigadier was accompanied on his guided tour by his wife's companion and she and Alfie Birtles laughed vigorously and obsequiously at his jokes. Mrs. Chichester Constable appeared towards the end of the visit in hat and coat and, we later learnt, told Mr. Birtles of her encounter with a ghostly presence soon after she came to live there. As the coach left, the Brigadier and the two ladies waved decorously and we waved back, ignoring Alfie Birtles' passionate plea to raise our caps. On the return journey he mused aloud over the good fortune of those born to riches.

I found it a disturbing, disorientating afternoon. I had had a glimpse of a way of life which had no relevance to anything I knew and it showed how limited was my vision. The view from the big house, I now realise, was also limited, and the private parkland distancing its occupants from the public highway was more than a matter of acreage. Once through the gate you had left Holderness and were in a place remote from its environment.

Wealth had allowed the Constables of the past to

view life from a vantage point inaccessible to other Holderness people, a privilege which isolated them because it was not shared. Even more divisively, as Catholics in an age when their minority religion was subject to social, political and penal discrimination, they were barred from important areas of English life. The chapel in the house and the discreetly concealed church at Marton were places of quiet mystery where most of their neighbours would have felt ill at ease.

Yorkshire people are too sensible and independent to be over-awed by their 'betters' and at the turn of the century the Lords Paramount of the Seigniory of Holderness were often referred to as the 'Teachester Constables'. Some time later, in the inter-war years, when there was a rare opportunity to go inside the Hall on some special occasion a number of female visitors defied prohibitions and sat briefly in a chair which had been lent to the Station Hotel in Hull to accommodate the royal bottom of Her late Majesty Queen Victoria on the occasion of her celebrated visit to Hull in 1854. The local press was not amused.

Purchase of an entry ticket now enables everyone to be a voyeur and to comment as frankly as they wish on things never intended for their eyes. But no modern tourist can be as tricky to handle as the acquisitive Queen Mary whose signed, framed photograph is prominently displayed on the bureaux and grand pianos of the Yorkshire mansions subjected to a royal visitation made in the course of a marauding expedition soon after the marriage of her daughter, the Princess Royal, to Lord Lascelles. Royal praise of an object was expected to be rewarded with an instant offer of whatever had taken the Queen's fancy, but the story goes that, before she arrived at Burton Constable, the owner of another house which had been a victim of Her Majesty's plunder forewarned the Chichester Constables of the technique she had perfected.

Consequently, when the Queen fixed her eyes on an item at Burton Constable and uttered the words which had previously been an open sesame to the fulfilment of her desires, 'We don't have one like that at Windsor,' she received the unanticipated rebuff, 'It's the only one we have at Burton Constable, ma'am.'

If the story isn't true, it deserves to be.

Burton Constable Hall contains treasures which even a queen could be tempted to covet and, as more rooms are opened, some very desirable objects are on view for the first time. One which used to be on show had a special attraction for me, although it had only modest value. It was a crimson and yellow banner bearing the device, 'Constable and Independence', which had played its part in the history of Hedon when Sir Thomas Aston Clifford Constable was elected an M.P. for the borough in 1830 – a rare piece of electoral ephemera for, although massive sums were spent by wealthy candidates on banners, flags, ribbons and favours (as well as food and drink) to please their supporters and intimidate opponents, in the rough and tumble of a contest the chances of survival were slim.

The fact that a Constable could stand as a parliamentary candidate in 1830 was a significant sign of progress. Members of the family had been M.P.s for Hedon in the 16th and 17th centuries but thereafter they were barred from Parliament on religious grounds until the passing of the Catholic Emancipation Act in 1829. Sir Thomas was only 23 and excluded from university (again as a Catholic), he had been educated on the Continent and had taken no part in public affairs. By temperament he was reserved and shy and it is more than likely that he had been morally blackmailed by the Hedon Town Clerk, James Iveson, who often pulled the strings controlling the activities of candidates and M.P.s, and who may have reminded the young baronet that duty required him to fulfil the obligations of the privileged station in life to which God had called him. A rowdy 19th-century election was an ordeal which would daunt the spirits of an extrovert and ambitious campaigner, but for a reluctant scion of the aristocracy, unaccustomed to close contact with the plebs, it must have been a nightmare.

The outward show was faultless. On election day, 30 July, 1830, a magnificent cavalcade left Burton Constable *en route* for Hedon, Sir Thomas and his lady in the leading landau, followed by a barouche and a carriage and pair, and, after them, a great number of open carriages and riders, three abreast. As they passed through the park and out into the country lanes, more carriages and riders joined the procession until there was a mile between Sir Thomas's landau and the last man on horseback. Farmhouses along the route were decorated with crimson and yellow flags, and loyal tenants at the roadside and in the villages cheered as he passed. The tail of the procession was still in Preston when Sir Thomas reached the boundary of Hedon, and there the horses were removed from his vehicle by supporters who hauled it into the Market Place, preceded by a band.

There were only two candidates for two seats and hardly any uncertainty about the outcome but at the nomination Sir Thomas shook like a leaf, probably terrified by the prospect of an honour about to be paid him. Once declared duly elected, he was placed in a ceremonial chair and carried through the streets on the shoulders of his minders, a hazardous journey and all a far cry from the secluded elegance of the Drawing Room at Burton Constable. He was now an M.P. but not for long. One year later, in 1831, Parliament was dissolved in the midst of a constitutional crisis over Reform and he was obliged to seek re-election. This time it was a mere formality, but a Pyrrhic victory, as the Reform Act of 1832 deprived Hedon, a notorious rotten borough, of its parliamentary representation, a change the locals bitterly resented but hardly unreasonable, with around 300 men, most of them non-resident, having the right to send two M.P.s to Westminster at a time when some of the rapidly expanding industrial towns of the North were unrepresented. At this point Sir Thomas Aston Clifford Constable Bart., deprived of his tiny supporting role on the national stage, withdrew into the much more congenial life-style of a landed gentleman.

I am pleased to see the more prominent position given to him and his wife in the newly revitalised Burton Constable. There were many compensations in no longer being an M.P. and their Continental travels gave them the opportunity to acquire rich and ornate French furniture to beautify and brighten Burton Constable.

The Hall is too far off the tourist track ever to attract the crowds who tramp round Blenheim, Chatsworth and Castle Howard but, under its new trust status and with the formation of the Friends of Burton Constable, there are plans to give it a higher profile. Its rarified atmosphere which was once disconcerting is now a refreshing antidote to the stresses of 20th-century living outside the park gates.

Withernsea sea front and bandstand. Winifred Holtby loved the bustling atmosphere of Withernsea and used it as the model for 'Kiplington' in South Riding.

Withernsea

Withernsea was ringed with magic. Foreign travel has downgraded English seaside resorts, particularly the smaller ones, into the poorest of relations, but, once the end of wartime restrictions turned dreams into reality, a visit to Withernsea offered all the pleasures one could expect this side of Heaven. More often, in fact, we went to Tunstall because it was quieter and more private; the sea and the sand were just as good and the scenery better but I longed for Withernsea and its heady metropolitan delights.

Yet, even the apparently endless ride to Tunstall had that thrilling moment when you caught a first glimpse of a sea that was always bluer than you expected. And the unmistakable prelude to journey's end was the toytown of bijou wooden bungalows and chalets which seemed to enhance, not mar, the landscape, and were coveted as desperately as if they had been villas on the Côte d'Azur.

Hornsea I did not really know until later and now prefer, but for children in our part of Holderness the mecca was Withernsea. Thomas Tindall Wildridge, author of the guide to the railway, had been even more enthusiastic when in 1884 he eulogised the superior merits of Withernsea air and sea: 'Come with me from north, south, or west, and I will lead to a quiet, unassuming village on the east coast of Yorkshire, where, whatever else may or may not be there found, health certainly will.... Stretching far out into the waters of the broad German Ocean, its breezes are more fresh and bracing than those of its compeers'.

It was very much a matter of chance that

Withernsea was ever chosen as the terminal point of the railway for, when the idea of a line linking Hull and the Holderness coast was first proposed, there was no particular reason why it should go to Withernsea; both Easington and Tunstall were considered before Withernsea was finally selected — and its entire future changed.

Before the coming of the railway Withernsea could be described unflatteringly but accurately as nothing more than 'a long straggling village on the sea cliff with 850 acres of land upon which the ocean encroaches nearly two yards every year'. To add to the depression was 'the ruined shell of a large and once beautiful church', St. Nicholas, which had been unroofed in a storm in 1609; since then it had remained 'a neglected ruin, the township having become too poor for the support of such a costly structure'.

Modern Withernsea owes its existence to Anthony Bannister, the visionary, idiosyncratic, but not too scrupulous promoter of the Hull and Holderness Railway (as it was originally called) and it is appropriate that a Withernsea street should bear his name. Withernsea was created in the wake of railway mania. If little fishing village in the south of England — like Brighton — could be converted by the railway into popular resorts for the Victorian masses, then, asked local men of enthusiasm who dreamed of vast dividends on their investments, why should they not repeat the success in East Yorkshire.

Their choice was a decision of destiny which transformed the whole appearance and character of the town, and the census of 1841, taken when Withernsea slumbered in anonymity, undisturbed by progress, is in marked contrast to that of 1861, seven years after the opening of the line. In 1841 Withernsea had a population of only 126 inhabiting 25 houses (by 1851 it had declined further to 109), but there was a high proportion of young people — 73 were 20 or under — and it was probably livelier than it sounds. Agriculture was the main activity,

A visit to a local seaside resort was an adventure – until the post-war period when foreign travel became popular.

Withernsea Lighthouse stands away from the coast and now houses a museum which includes an exhibition on Kay Kendall, the Withernsea-born film star.

and the small community included 11 farmers and eight labourers as well as the six male and four female servants they employed. It is certain, too, that the children formed an essential (and unpaid) labour force for the family farms. A mere handful of people were not involved in farming — a shoemaker, a female grocer, a tailor (who had a schoolmaster lodging with him), a publican, a boatman and an elderly woman who, in the blunt phraseology of pre-Welfare State days, was described as a pauper.

Twenty years later it was a very different picture. The town had experienced a meteoric growth for, although Withernsea itself is recorded as having a population of only 202, the development of the part of the town which fell within the parish of Owthorne was separately recorded in the census. There were now 424 people in Owthorne, making a total population of 626, and a directory summarises the story of Withernsea's expansion: 'Many good houses and shops with several inns have been built within the last three years for the accommodation of the numerous visitors who resort thither during the bathing season.'

Apart from the railway station itself, the most notable building in the town was the Queen's Hotel (now the hospital) erected at a cost of £10,530 and designed by Cuthbert Brodrick who was employed as the railway architect. Both hotel and station were 'well lighted' with gas from the Railway Company's own works. The intention was to attract a distinguished and refined clientèle. 'The Queen's

Hotel,' states the railway guide, 'stands in pleasant grounds and affords a beautiful view of the sea. Possibly Withernsea and the surrounding country is viewed under no more favourable aspect than from the windows of the Hotel.' An advertisement in the same publication described it as 'unsurpassed by any other Hotel on the coast; charges most reasonable, cuisine, wines and spirits of the best quality,' and listed amongst its amenities a ladies' drawing room, an elegant coffee room, a billiard and smoke room and a lawn tennis court. In 1861 the hotel keeper was Mrs. Ann Varley, a widow assisted by her son and daughter and a formidable army of downstairs staff: a housekeeper, cook, chambermaid, kitchenmaid, waiter, laundry maid – down to the humble Boots. They were ready for the influx of business which, alas, never came on the scale they anticipated, though in 1861 the nine visitors staying at the Queen's included George Johnson, a landed proprietor, and Thomas White, the Hull fruit merchant.

It is much easier to write the history of a place than to forecast its future. Anthony Bannister's high hopes for Withernsea were not fulfilled, and fashionable visitors did not appear in adequate numbers to make the Queen's Hotel a profitable

Pierrots were a popular feature on the beach at Withernsea. Great skill was needed to make your escape before the collecting-box reached you.

concern. In 1862 the independent Hull and Holderness Railway was taken over by the N.E.R. The town did, however, establish its distinctive character at a very early stage. 'Withernsea seems to possess a special fascination,' wrote a journalist of the Edwardian period trying to analyse the subtle distinction of styles between east coast resorts. 'There is something stern and wild about Withernsea and a spirit of freedom.'

Although Withernsea obviously disappointed the Victorian railway entrepreneurs who had visions of fame and fortune, it is a seaside resort which has a secure place in many people's affections. For many, a day at Withernsea provided the most exciting and memorable social event of the year, and the apparently endless journey involved in getting there by horse-drawn vehicles on an outing increased the thrill of anticipation and tension.

For my mother, living on an isolated farm at Little Humber, a day at Withernsea had been an even rarer treat than it was for me and she described the thrill of such an adventure in *Back of Beyond:*

'There was also an annual outing to Withernsea. My mother would take us on the trip and we had to be at the village by 7.00 a.m. which meant leaving home at 6.00 a.m. In the village there would be two or three wagons and horses ready, all done up with brasses and ribbons. Every wagon or rully – seats were put on them for the passengers - was full with mothers and children and it was a great success.

'It was a slow ride and we seemed ages getting there so excitement would mount. We would arrive before midday and spend most of our time on the sands. There were donkeys, a Punch and Judy show and I think there were pierrots – there certainly were in later years. You were supposed to pay for the performance by putting something in a collection, but a lot of us sneaked away before we were approached. The last hour we went round the shops and always brought something home as a souvenir. I once bought a little doll in a bath and, of course, we never came back without a stick of Withernsea rock.

We would leave for home about 6.00 p.m. and what a joyful ride it was. We would sing and laugh and on this occasion did not mind how long it took us to get back. Usually it would be about 10.30 p.m. by the time we reached the village and my father would be there to meet us with the horse and trap and we arrived back home about 11 o'clock or so, really tired out.'

To be part of the childhood memories of so many local people is an enviable role for any town – and one in which Withernsea should continue to take great pride.

Spurn Point

No reason is needed for a visit to Spurn Point. You go because it's there, and it is an achievement to have been. Everything about it is unlikely and in defiance of logic and commonsense: a narrow strip of land which reaches recklessly into the North Sea much farther than anyone has the right to expect and which seems longer each time you travel along the sandy road, though there is always a sense of disappointment when at last you reach the end. If it can go as far as this, why not go on for ever? On a map Spurn Point looks nothing more than the accidental track of a cartographer's wandering pen, but film taken from the air is dramatic evidence of land hanging precariously by a thread, enough to make you feel rather proud that you had the courage to attempt such a fearsome expedition.

I am not sure if I was taken to Spurn when visiting relations joined a family group on an outing there just before the War. I have no personal memories but this was a day on which grown-ups reminisced so often that their anecdotes become confused with first-hand observations. It was a very hot day and my uncle caused quite a stir by wearing a white topi which we had been given. He and his sister, both teachers, were intrigued when they heard Spurn Point children singing in such extreme dialect that they were reminded of a Scandinavian folk song, not surprisingly in a region which has been repeatedly colonised by invaders from northern Europe.

During the war Spurn was under strict military control, and, for years after, journey's end was Kilnsea, where a barrier as impenetrable as the Berlin Wall blocked your way to what lay beyond. In 1960 it was acquired by the Yorkshire Naturalists Trust as a nature reserve and visits became possible, but it is only in recent years that it has intrigued me more and more.

It is quite a long way to Patrington, but then the journey into deepest Holderness really begins as

Spurn Point and its lighthouse, built 1895.

The railway built in the First World War, which operated between Kilnsea and Spurn Point.

you travel along a road winding uncertainly through vast hedgeless fields, past homely villages and largish but unostentatious farmhouses, like distant oases, rooted in the earth and protected by a screen of mature trees from biting easterly breezes. And over it all the overwhelming skies of Holderness and their constant reminder that this mundane world is part of something vast and mysterious.

Until recently the best way of travelling into the farthest corner of south-east Holderness was by Connor & Graham's bus, a vintage village bus service with all the pleasures of listening in to the local gossip, hearing an informed commentary on the passing scene, and being for a short time a member of a closed community of pioneers who had ventured out into the wide world and were now returning to the security of home. But the terminus was the old Blue Bell at Kilnsea, and after that it was the endless walk to Spurn Point – or as far as you could go before it was time to turn back. On one of these walks I saw Michael Clegg, the TV naturalist, lying on the ground at the entrance to the Warren, waiting with cheerful patience for the right moment to take a photograph of a bird to use as a slide illustration in one of his talks.

To stand at the very tip and watch the swirling

Crest on the premises of the Humber Pilots. The three crowns of Kingston upon Hull are a reminder that the Lord Mayor is Admiral of the Humber. The Latin motto means 'Always Ready'.

Families at Spurn Point have always led a lonely life and a teacher at the school which was formerly there commented that some children had never seen common animals or trees.

waters where the Humber meets the North Sea is worth all the effort and inconvenience of getting there, and the satisfaction of achievement is made all the more exhilarating by fresh winds driving at your face and allowing you to imagine that you are no passive tourist but a real traveller who has beaten a way through obstacles to reach the very edge of the world.

If Spurn is unbelievable, it takes even more credulity and imagination to stand at the Point and realise that ever farther out in these dangerous waters was once the prosperous island port of Ravenser Odd. It was not mentioned in Domesday Book but was formed by the North Sea forcing its way through the narrow peninsular to meet the Humber. The rise of Ravenser Odd was a blow to Hedon, and, when an inquiry into Hedon's finances was held in 1280, there was a dispirited moan that the men of Hedon were impoverished on account of two good harbours which were daily increasing: Ravenser Odd and Wyke – or Hull as it became. So much had Ravenser Odd grown that, in 1299, Edward I granted charters to both Hull and Ravenser Odd in identical terms though Hull, more favoured by the King, paid only a cut-price 100 marks for its privileges, a bargain compared with the 300 marks exacted from the merchants of Ravenser Odd.

How difficult it is to believe that beneath the waves was a thriving community which sent two M.P.s to Westminster, for the factor which had been its greatest asset, its accessibility to shipping coming up the Humber, led to its demise. Ravenser Odd was extremely vulnerable in a period when Holderness suffered even more disastrously than it does at present from the ravages of the North Sea. The 1340s were a time of appalling weather, with fierce storms and abnormally high tides, and the Humber flooded the land as far as Cottingham and Anlaby. Ravenser Odd could not survive and, like the more romantically named lost villages of Tharlesthorpe, Frismersk, Penisthorpe, Orwithfleet, East Somerte and Sunthorpe, it disappeared into the oblivion from which it had emerged. The bells of its church were salvaged in time and sold to Easington and Aldbrough, and the bodies removed for re-burial at Easington. Spurn leaves few visitors unimpressed, and, when Sir George Head included it in his itinerary of a tour through the manufacturing districts of England, in 1835, he pondered on the 'dreary and awful' fate of those condemned to live in such fearful circumstances, a melancholy mood re-inforced by the pathetic plots of barren gardens in front of the lifeboat crew's cottages.

John Redwood Anderson, a Hymers College master, once regarded as an important poet, knew Holderness well and in 1940 published a book, *The Curlew Cries*, which, prophetically, contained a series of poems called 'Humberside', one entitled *Spurn Light* and one *April in Holderness.*

In more recent times a much better poet, Philip Larkin, conveyed in fewer but more powerful words his sensitivity to the unique atmosphere of this remote corner of England where silence stands like heat.

Some people find Holderness dull and too flat for their liking. But for me the great skies of Holderness, the Dutch-like scenery and the sense of separation from the madding crowd create an atmosphere which is soothing and seductive. A trip into Holderness is a therapeutic experience in an age of turmoil.

The reluctant rector Dr. John Hymers

In the Forties and Fifties churches and chapels of all denominations just plodded on, making a minor concession to modernity here and there but not yet disturbed by the theological and spiritual revolution which would soon disturb the comfortable, challenge mindless routine, and let in light. Church magazines of the time convey a picture of a Holderness which seems quite remote: separate small parishes each with its own rector or vicar, usually a graduate. It was hardly demanding work, and the Anglican parson's freehold gave him the security of life tenure and an independence which was conducive to the development of eccentricity.

Although I eventually learnt that Hymers College, the school I attended in Hull, was founded by John Hymers, it was much later when I realised that he belonged to a long tradition of Anglican scholar-clergymen, isolated among rustics, whose guaranteed income and virtual immunity from dismissal encouraged habits and attitudes which at times were decidedly strange.

When news reached Brandesburton in 1852 that Dr. John Hymers had been appointed Rector the people in the village probably wondered what sort of a chap they were getting. A 19th-century clergyman was an important figure in a Holderness rural community and his influence spread far beyond the village church.

Brandesburton Rectory was for 35 years the home of the introverted and unhappy Dr. John Hymers, who added a library – and amassed a fortune which he left in a faulty home-made will to 'found and endow' a school.

Whatever the rumours that passed round Brandesburton in 1852, the reality proved far stranger than any expectations. Hymers was the proverbial square peg fitting awkwardly in a very round hole and no one realised his unsuitability for the position more quickly than Hymers himself.

The new rector was a bachelor in his 50th year, a theologian and mathematician, who had spent the past 30 years at Cambridge and, now, at a time when unwelcome change was in the air at his beloved university, he had made the monumental blunder of resigning his post as President of St. John's College and becoming Rector of Brandesburton, one of the richest livings in its patronage, with what was then the magnificent annual income of £1,500.

Hymers was no stranger to country life and there was nothing affluent about his background. His grandfather and father were farmers in North Yorkshire and he made his own way through Cambridge, working with great application to win a series of scholarships which raised him not far above the poverty line.

But the long years in academia had taken him far from his roots. He had reached the upper échelons of the University and he had lost any ability he ever had to communicate with ordinary people. He arrived at Brandesburton Rectory, a pleasant, spacious house with an attractive garden in a most agreeable rural setting, an ideal family home but large and lonely for a middle-aged bachelor who missed the scholarly environment so congenial to a man of his interests and temperament. He tried to return to Cambridge but his post had been filled, and he and Brandesburton were stuck with each other for the next 35 years.

It was not a happy situation. Hymers was unpopular in the village and his parishioners regarded him as mean and penny-pinching, criticising him for being 'near' in financial matters, insisting on tithes being paid down to the last farthing, depriving local tradesmen of employment by doing jobs at the Rectory himself and, instead of following the country code of giving away surplus produce, charging them for the rhubarb he could not eat. His stock phrase, 'Three sticks a penny', became the joke of Brandesburton, the ultimate proof of the miserliness of their eccentric Rector.

The reputation for stinginess which he attracted was not the whole truth. Secretly Hymers helped many individuals and, when he sat as a J.P., he sometimes fulfilled his duty by fining a man, but quietly paid the fine himself, and he would hold out

Dr. John Hymers. The unhappy Rector of Brandesburton whose financial astuteness made him a great educational benefactor.

against fellow magistrates who wanted to impose a sentence which he considered harsh. Beneath the cold exterior there was, no doubt, a man of goodwill who desperately longed for affection but who was too inhibited to reveal the warmth of feeling submerged beneath a manner which repelled.

Nor was he particularly good at his official duties. Like other Cambridge Fellows, he had been ordained, but he had no previous experience in a parish, he was a poor preacher and, apart from Communion, left his curate, Rev. J. F. Wilkinson, to conduct all services. St. Mary's Church was neglected, the walls crumbled, the interior was mildewed, and nettles and weeds obstructed the entrance.

Yet there were points in his favour. He bought a harmonium and new hymn and psalm books, and he entertained the Sunday School to splendid dinners in the Rectory kitchens where the menu included monster joints of beef, massive – and over-rich – plum puddings, and ale.

Although Brandesburton hardly vied with Cambridge, he maintained his interest in education, personally testing the children on the Catechism and reprimanding parents who sent their children to school poorly dressed; afterwards he gave them the money to put matters right. He also built a village library (said to be large enough for a football match), open every evening except Sunday.

Hymers found solace in reading and by the time of his death had amassed a collection of 6,000 books. He kept a good stable and loved riding and driving, but he was also an enthusiast for the new railways and travelled widely. More significantly for posterity, he invested shrewdly in railway preference shares and, with a growing capital and an income too large for his needs, became one of the major property owners in the area, buying land, farms, cottages and even a blacksmith's shop.

This expanding business empire was controlled from his study at the rear of the house where he sat at a table facing the outer door, keeping an eye on the school opposite and strategically positioned to prevent anyone taking him by surprise. He occupied the sole chair in the room and there was a memorable occasion when a gentleman farmer who resented being made to stand while the Rector sat took his revenge by meting out the same treatment when Hymers later visited his house.

Hymers was fortunate in having his spinster niece, Esther Jackson, willing to act as his housekeeper but the high turnover of servants indicates that domestic life at Brandesburton Rectory did not run smoothly. The lonely house was furnished in sombre style but the cellar was amply stocked with vintage wines. He had transferred to Brandesburton the alcoholic habits of a 19th-century don and his journal shows that he accepted the link between his later illnesses and his over-indulgence. At his death in 1887 the cellar contained 145 dozen bottles of fine wine.

By now he was a man of considerable wealth, and his personal estate was valued at around £170,000. As a self-made man wishing to acknowledge his debt to education, he had decided to leave the bulk of his fortune to establish a grammar school in Hull but, with staggering stupidity, he did not consult a lawyer and wrote out his own will. His reluctance to employ others resulted in a fatal error in its wording, the bequest was invalid and his brother, Robert, became the beneficiary. Robert did, however, agree to donate £50,000 of his unexpected windfall to found a school and Hymers College was opened in 1893.

John Hymers' 35 years in Holderness is a story of loneliness, frustration and wasted ability which had even more appalling consequences for himself than for his unfortunate parishioners. Life, though, is full of irony. Out of all the unhappiness came a distinguished school and in its centenary year, 1993, hundreds of Hymerians, past and present, both male and female, made a pilgrimage to Brandesburton to honour a man whose failings can now be forgiven and whose good works live on.

A Holderness Murder

Crime, contrary to what some imagine, was not unknown a century or more ago, but murder was less likely in the countryside than in a crowded city. All the more horror — and fascination — therefore when a violent crime was committed in the parish of Preston in Holderness at the end of July, 1891. It was a crime I had been told about before I found the lengthy accounts of the murder in an old newspaper, and for me it has a particular personal interest.

Sherlock Holmes stories and even real Victorian murders have acquired a period flavour from the glimpse they give of a way of life so different from our own, though incidents which make enthralling reading often had a brutality which the passing of time has tended to blur. Mary Jane Langley certainly met a brutal end. She was 19 years old and lived with her parents at Westfield Farm, one of three farms in Preston Long Lane, by which it could be reached from Marfleet Station on the Hull-Withernsea line.

On Thursday, 30 July, her parents had left the farm at noon, put up their trap in Great Union Street, Hull, and walked to Paragon Station to take the train to Driffield. Mary Jane was not expected to be away from home in their absence and they were naturally astonished when they returned at half-past six and found her missing.

Time passed and they persuaded themselves that she had gone to Hull to visit friends or even crossed over to Cleethorpes as her father had previously refused her permission to go there with her sweetheart. Her brother revealed that, soon after seeing her parents off, she had told him that she was going to Hull to have her photograph taken and would be back in time to take the men their 'allowance' in the fields. 'She was known as a very steady, dutiful young woman and her parents did not apprehend her falling into evil company', and consequently they were still not unduly alarmed.

Concern grew when she failed to appear the

My great grandfather, Sergeant John Sales, with his wife, Hannah (née Peach), his eldest daughter, Martha, and his only son, Arthur.

following morning. Mr. Langley decided to wait no longer and started his own inquiries in Hull. It was confirmed that she had visited a photographer in Witham, it later transpired that she had been spotted the previous afternoon near the Jewish Cemetery on Hedon Road and, more significantly, that she had been seen alighting from the train at Marfleet and climbing over a stile to take a footpath that led to Preston.

When Friday evening came with no further news, Mr. Langley resolved to return to Hull once again. He was walking along the lane to Marfleet, which he always dreaded because of its loneliness, when he noticed a retriever following a scent into a ditch through a brick archway connecting the roadway and the field. He walked on, made an abortive visit to Hull and, at last, the following afternoon, made up his mind (surely not before time) to obtain a copy of Mary Jane's recent photograph and take it to the police. Once again he noticed the same dog behaving oddly in the same place. Mr. Langley climbed on to a gate leading into a wheat field and there, at the bottom of a ditch, he saw the body of his daughter.

Victorian journalists considered it appropriate to treat incidents of violent death with great solemnity and the local press recorded the victim's wounds in dread detail. It concluded, 'All the circumstances pointed clearly to murder but as to the perpetrator of the ghastly deed there is up to the present time no clue, and the police appear to be altogether in the dark in the elucidation of the mystery.'

Dr. James Soutter was summoned and Superintendent Burniston of the Sproatley Police informed. News of the murder spread rapidly, and a visit to the scene of the crime proved a highly popular Bank Holiday weekend outing, 'gossiping knots of inhabitants assembled at almost every point', and amateur detectives were quick to air their theories. There were those who thought Miss Langley had been murdered by someone she knew, but the majority opinion was that it must have been a man from Hull. It was well-known that a number of men from the Southcoates district 'made it a practice to visit the country by these by-lanes bent on pleasures peculiar to themselves'.

And at last a likely culprit came into focus, a man wearing light-coloured trousers who had been drinking at the Nag's Head, Preston, that Thursday afternoon, accompanied by his dog, and who had been seen later near the place where the body was found. This prime suspect was quickly identified as a local hero, John Rennard, known as 'Jack Renny' to his friends in Hull's boxing fraternity, the winner of several bouts against celebrated middle-weight champions, though his behaviour had become erratic after a fight earlier in the year, particularly when he had been drinking.

On Monday morning Detective Sergeant Rutherford and Sergeant John Sales located Rennard in a Holderness Road dram shop, accompanied him to his house in Courtney Street, and Sergeant Sales went upstairs with him into the front bedroom where he handed over the moleskin trousers he had been wearing on the Thursday. They were stained with blood, and Sergeant Sales informed Rennard he would be arrested and charged with murder.

He was brought up before the Petty Sessions and the case adjourned for a week. Its resumption aroused excitement bordering on hysteria. In court there was standing room only and hundreds crowded outside in a futile attempt to get a glimpse of something interesting.

Sergeant Sales was cross-examined about the discovery of the moleskin trousers:

'Whilst you were examining the blood marks on his trousers did he change his countenance?'

'Yes, he changed colour.'

'You actually saw him turn pale?'

'Yes, his lips were tremulous.'

It seemed an open-and-shut case but, in spite of blood on the trousers and also on a handkerchief, the Borough Analyst was unable to confirm that it was human, a matter on which a modern forensic scientist would be much more forthcoming.

In the circumstances the magistrates considered they had no real evidence and Rennard was discharged. It was an immensely popular decision, he was the hero of the hour, and his heftier admirers released the horse from the shafts of a cab and conveyed him home in triumph.

The case remained unsolved, and who killed Mary Jane Langley will never be known. But there is a sequel. Sergeant John Sales was my great-grandfather and to the end of his life he was convinced he had arrested the right man.

Town and country meet near Salt End

Winifred Holtby and *South Riding*

South Riding was still news in the post-war years. Books and paper were scarce, Winifred Holtby's best-seller had been published only in 1936, with the film of the book following in 1937, and in 1940, the first year of war, Vera Brittain's *Testament of Friendship* .

The novel dealt with a decade not long past and, although local historians were not as thick on the ground as they are in the 1990s, there were many readers who recognised a very close likeness between characters and events in the book and real-life counterparts, a resemblance that caused the author's mother, Alderman Mrs. Alice Holtby, great embarrassment and probably led to her resignation from the East Riding County Council and retirement in Harrogate.

It's something I read at the crucial adolescent stage of life when a book can have an impact from which you never recover. I have reread it several times since and I still see it as the near perfect picture of a Holderness which just lingered on when I was young.

It is a waste of time looking for the South Riding on a map – even one printed in pre-Humberside days – but residents of Holderness can pride themselves on living in the area which Winifred Holtby chose to transform into the fictional South Riding. For Winifred Holtby, born at Rudston near Bridlington

Typical 'South Riding' countryside near Sunk Island, the area Winifred Holtby called 'Cold Harbour Colony'.

in 1898, the Yorkshire Wolds were the English countryside at its best, and it may seem strange that she should set her great story of rural life, not in her native Wolds, but in Holderness, a district of quite different scenery and atmosphere.

Yet, the circumstances in which the book was conceived and written provide the explanation. By 1931 Winifred had established a high reputation as a journalist and author, but the dazzling future which she had every reason to expect was cruelly snatched from her when she became ill and Bright's Disease was diagnosed. Excellent medical advice enabled her to keep going and it was in 1934 that she decided to find a quiet place on the Yorkshire coast where she could work in peace, safe from all the demands of her hectic London life.

She advertised in the *Hull Daily Mail* and was offered accommodation which suited her needs, a furnished house, Delma, now 27 Waxholme Road, Withernsea, at a rent of ten shillings a week, with the advantage of a woman living opposite who had seven daughters and who would arrange to 'do' for her daily.

Once settled in Withernsea, Winifred enjoyed her morning walks on the beach and along the coast, while afternoons were usually spent writing her book, *Women and a Changing Civilisation.* She did reviews, and visitors could always recognise the house by the piles of new books on the window sill. But, most important of all, she was collecting the impressions which were later to be incorporated in *South Riding.* The idea for the novel had come to her earlier, but Withernsea gave it shape. 'The town may be ugly but it has beauties of its own,' she told her best friend, Vera Brittain. On another occasion she revealed how her mind was working: 'One day I must write about Withernsea, the town everybody wants to leave.'

Although other East Coast resorts made their contribution, most of the inspiration for 'Kiplington' came from Withernsea, and passages in *South Riding* show how deep was her affection for it. 'It was a perfect July evening,' one description begins. 'The little town swam in warm liquid light.' The two months spent in Withernsea from mid-April to mid-June in 1934 were a fruitful period. A novelist's brain is never off duty, and, as well as the long walks, there were local journeys in which she noticed people, places and scenes which could be woven into the novel forming in her mind.

Quite possibly on a train journey between Withernsea and Hull she caught a glimpse of the shuttered and creeper-covered White Hall at Winestead. On a sketch map of *South Riding* which she prepared before starting to write, and which had fictional names superimposed on an outline of Holderness, the location of 'Maythorpe' coincide with Winestead. Yorkshire Television made a

Holy Trinity Church, Sunk Island, a fine Victorian church, surprisingly sophisticated for such a remote area. Now redundant and a heritage centre, it houses an exhibition on Winifred Holtby whose descriptions of Sunk Island are the most elegiac passages in South Riding.

Sunk Island consists of land risen from the waters of the Humber and, as such, is Crown land. 19th-century houses bear the insignia of Queen Victoria and the Prince Consort.

perfect choice when they used the White Hall for filming the scenes at 'Maythorpe Hall'.

It is, a mistake to look in a novel for exact descriptions of real places. As a writer of fiction Winifred had total freedom to draw on all her experiences, and 'Maythorpe Hall' must owe something to Dowthorpe Hall at Skirlaugh, where she spent childhood holidays at the home of her Uncle Tom, many of whose stories of Holderness

life became the raw material of *South Riding.*

Winifred's first love was the Wolds, but the undramatic yet distinctive atmosphere of Sunk Island with its thousands of lonely acres reclaimed from the Humber appealed to her imagination. Some of the most poetic passages in *South Riding* are those in which she conveys the strangely seductive atmosphere of 'The wide Dutch landscape, haunted by larks and seabirds . . . The loneliness, the silence, the slow inevitable rhythm of the tides'.

Fiction was not far removed from fact when Winifred created 'Cold Harbour Colony' and based the story of its struggle to survive on events still fresh in the minds of Holderness people. After the First World War a completely unrealistic scheme attempted to convert farmland into smallholdings for ex-servicemen. The project was doomed to failure, and local talk of the disastrous experiment at Sunk Island found a permanent literary outlet in the troubled history of 'Cold Harbour Colony'.

Away from Withernsea, Winifred began writing *South Riding* but illness intervened, and in February, 1935, she decided to return to the East Coast and find another quiet spot where she could recuperate and work. This time she chose Hornsea, but, as no suitable house was available, she took lodgings with the Misses Brooks at what is now 71 Cliff Road.

Domestic arrangements were fine but there were too many calls on her time from public speaking engagements and family commitments. News from abroad was increasing anxiety, and the sight and sound of planes on target practice over the sea were portents of the war she had campaigned so vigorously to prevent but which now seemed inevitable.

Winifred Holtby died in London on 29 September, 1935, and was buried in the churchyard at Rudston on 2 October. She had finished *South Riding* but it was left to Vera Brittain to see it through the press. It was published in 1936 to great acclaim. Versions have been made for the cinema and radio as well as television, and the book has never been out of print.

Interest in Winifred Holtby is now world-wide but *South Riding* will always have a special, more personal significance for people in Holderness. Anyone who wants to learn – or revive memories – of life in the area in the 1930s has only to turn the pages of this book which captures it all, just as it was.

Vivid yellow fields of rape have altered the Holderness landscape in recent years, but a traveller on the upper deck of a bus from Hull to Withernsea will still recognise the loving description of Sarah Burton's journey between 'Kingsport' and 'Kiplington': 'From point to point on the horizon her eye could pick out the clustering trees and dark spire or tower marking a village.'

Yorkshire, in reality, has only three Ridings, East, North and West, but none is more famous than the one that never existed.

Tetley's shire geldings hauling a dray in 1945.

Postscript

Writing about people and places you have known is not just a literary exercise. It re-creates the past, things you have not thought about for years come miraculously into focus, and you experience it all as if it were happening for the first time. The past becomes the present.

Sometimes, of course, it is disturbing to re-awaken dormant memories but, fortunately, happiness far outshines things less pleasant to remember and what I do not wish to include I have omitted. My impressions of Hedon and Holderness will not always be the same as yours, but I hope we shall not be divided in our love for what is one of the most individual and least known parts of England.